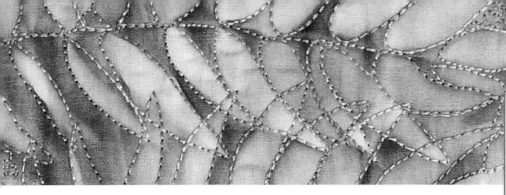

9

77

Published by:
Sulky of America, Inc.
© 2011 All Rights Reserved

980 Cobb Place Blvd. • Kennesaw, GA 30144
www.sulky.com

Express yourself with **sulky**®
Decorative Thread, Stabilizers & Books

Edited by: Fred Drexler and Patti Lee
Graphic Art: Dave Fingerlos

Library of Congress Catalogue Number:
ISBN # 978-1-931176-15-6
Printed in USA

59

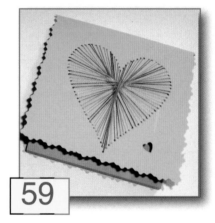

Follow us on Facebook
http://www.facebook.com/pages/
Sulky-of-America/109074659126806

Using your smartphone,* scan this tag to find out more about Blendables thread and other exciting products and events from Sulky. Try it!
*requires free app from http://gettag.mobi.com

99

W9-BPJ-078

1

I want to thank all of you who have enjoyed using Sulky products and books during the last three decades. It has been my pleasure to bring you hundreds of projects from so many talented contributors through the Sulky book series.

And now, it is my turn to introduce you to Sulky 100% Cotton Blendables® and Solid Color Threads. I have to admit that I am addicted to fabrics and have quite the stash in my studio in NC. The beautiful batiks, mottled solids and awesome prints inspired me to create the Blendables line of cotton thread in two weights for Sulky and your favorite independent Quilting and Sewing shops.

It was quite the tedious process developing the Blendables line of thread in 2005-2006. I worked from our 40 wt. Rayon line of colors, combining groups of five colors or shades together by sewing them individually in 1 inch increments. You can't imagine my excitement when the first batch of 42 colors arrived from the Sulky plant. Since this process had never been done before, we could only cross our fingers that the colors would turn out like those I had chosen. My first attempt was a roaring success, and your response to them was overwhelming, to say the least!

So, of course, in 2007-2008 we had to make more color choices. I got to fill in all the color ranges that I couldn't do the first time around. 42 new color combinations had to be picked and tested. It was so much fun experimenting and checking out fabric color trends so you would have the best selection possible in the second 42 shades. I created multi-colors and shades of similar colors combined. Because the colors change so rapidly and randomly in little bits of thread at a time, the impact on the fabrics was awesome. And, to make your creative juices flow even more, Sulky has 66 coordinating solid color cottons in both 12 wt. and 30 wt.

Because you asked for it, during the last year I developed 42 more incredible color combinations. After you see all of the dazzling and amazing ways to use Blendables in this book, you will want to own all 126 colors in both 12 wt. and 30 wt. Enjoy using this book that features many of your favorite designers showing you how versatile this thread can be for hand work, quilting, crafting, serging, embroidery and more.

Visit www.sulky.com for more information, including FREE projects! Check out our new Sulky Embroidery Club at www.sulkyembclub.com for designs from Carol Ingram and me. Plus, be sure to sign up for my informative and FREE Monthly Newsletter at www.sulky.com.

Create with Confidence,

Joyce Drexler

Joyce Drexler
Author, Artist, Designer,
T.V. Personality and
co-founder of
Sulky of America

Because you asked for them - Introducing ...

42 More Blendables®

Stunningly beautiful, all new, must-have Blendables!

All are available on King-Size, Snap-End Spools that contain 330 yds. of 12 wt. and 500 yds. of 30 wt.! Sulky Blendables are now available in 126 colors exclusively at independent retail stores.

- Highest quality, long staple 100% Egyptian Cotton.

- A masterful blend of different colors within the same range of tone and intensity. Random color changes every 2-1/2" to 5".

- Ideal for Quilting, Appliquéing, Serging and Embroidering Batiks, Mottled Solids, Florals or any Multi-Colored or Shaded Fabric.

- You'll be amazed at how each "Blendable" will work perfectly with so many different-colored fabrics.

- Blending effects are like nothing you have ever seen before.

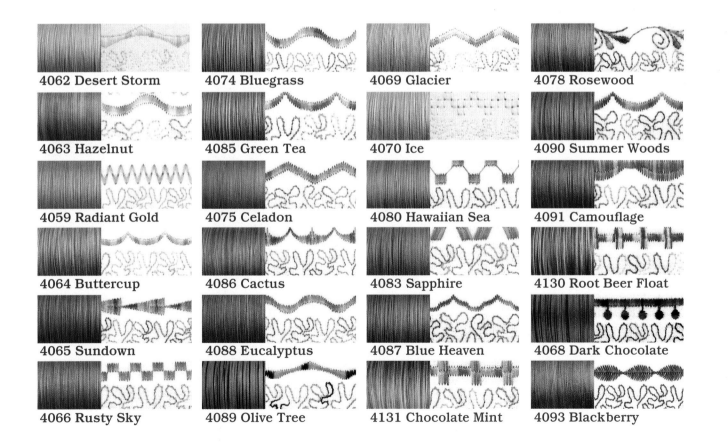

4062 Desert Storm   4074 Bluegrass   4069 Glacier   4078 Rosewood

4063 Hazelnut   4085 Green Tea   4070 Ice   4090 Summer Woods

4059 Radiant Gold   4075 Celadon   4080 Hawaiian Sea   4091 Camouflage

4064 Buttercup   4086 Cactus   4083 Sapphire   4130 Root Beer Float

4065 Sundown   4088 Eucalyptus   4087 Blue Heaven   4068 Dark Chocolate

4066 Rusty Sky   4089 Olive Tree   4131 Chocolate Mint   4093 Blackberry

Stunningly Beautiful

4092 Summer Fruit

4058 Primrose

4079 Hyacinth

4071 Pale Amethyst

4060 Tangerine Morning

4077 Seaside Sun

4084 Twilight

4072 Lavender Fields

4061 Poppy

4129 Beachwood

4081 Passion Fruit

4073 Lilac Meadow

4132 Hat Ladies

4076 Breeze

4082 Wild Rose

4094 Granite

4067 Merlot Blush

4128 Neon Lights

Save Big with Sulky Universal Slimline Box Assortments

30 wt. Blendables Starter Package
Art. 886-09 17 Popular Colors

30 wt. Blendables Dream Package
Art. 886-11 42 Original Colors

30 wt. Blendables Dream Package
Art. 886-13 42 Colors/2nd Collection

12 wt. Blendables Starter Package
Art. 886-08 17 Popular Colors

12 wt. Blendables Dream Package
Art. 886-10 42 Original Colors

12 wt. Blendables Dream Package
Art. 886-12 42 Colors/2nd Collection

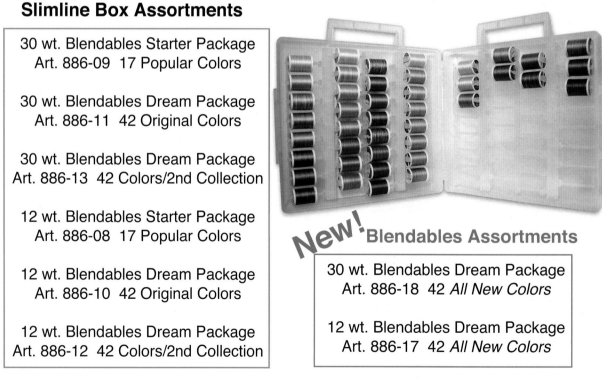

New! **Blendables Assortments**

30 wt. Blendables Dream Package
Art. 886-18 42 *All New Colors*

12 wt. Blendables Dream Package
Art. 886-17 42 *All New Colors*

Ask your favorite independent retailer to order an assortment for you.

4

Original 84 Blendables®

 4001 Parchment

 4125 Butter & Sky

 4049 Melon Soft

 4057 Fresh Butter

 4012 Baby Soft

 4013 Sun & Sea

 4026 Earth Pastels

 4002 Buttercream

 4048 Gentle Hues

 4015 Cool Waters

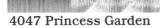 4102 Spring Garden

 4040 Biscuit

 4103 Pansies

 4016 Peacock Plume

 4047 Princess Garden

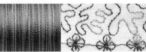 4044 Butterscotch

 4024 Heather

 4021 Truly Teal

 4127 Summer Garden

 4003 Sunset

 4025 Hydrangea

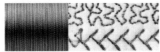 4110 Light Jewels

 4029 Mocha Mauve

 4004 Golden Flame

 4046 Sweet Rose

 4032 Iris

 4122 Rosebud Sweet

 4006 Autumn

 4030 Vintage Rose

 4111 Deep Jewels

4101 Easter Eggs

4117 Fall Holidays

4005 Strawberry Daiquiri

 4033 Grape Wine

4041 Fiesta

4010 Carmel Apple

 4008 Peach Parfait

4126 Basic Brights

4124 Summertime

4011 Milk Chocolate

 4043 Tropical

4104 Christmas Trio

4115 Wildflowers

 4038 Deep Woods

Beautifully Multi-Colored

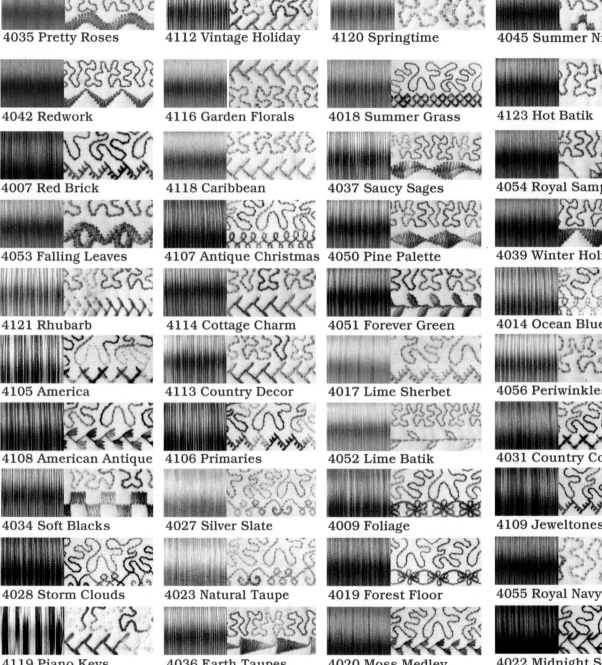

4035 Pretty Roses	4112 Vintage Holiday	4120 Springtime	4045 Summer Nights
4042 Redwork	4116 Garden Florals	4018 Summer Grass	4123 Hot Batik
4007 Red Brick	4118 Caribbean	4037 Saucy Sages	4054 Royal Sampler
4053 Falling Leaves	4107 Antique Christmas	4050 Pine Palette	4039 Winter Holidays
4121 Rhubarb	4114 Cottage Charm	4051 Forever Green	4014 Ocean Blue
4105 America	4113 Country Decor	4017 Lime Sherbet	4056 Periwinkles
4108 American Antique	4106 Primaries	4052 Lime Batik	4031 Country Colonial
4034 Soft Blacks	4027 Silver Slate	4009 Foliage	4109 Jeweltones
4028 Storm Clouds	4023 Natural Taupe	4019 Forest Floor	4055 Royal Navy
4119 Piano Keys	4036 Earth Taupes	4020 Moss Medley	4022 Midnight Sky

For 12 wt. Cotton Blendables, a 16/100 Topstitch or Denim Needle is recommended.
For 30 wt. Cotton Blendables, a 14/90 Topstitch or Denim Needle is recommended.

66 Sulky Solid Color Cottons

Premier quality, long staple, highly mercerized Egyptian Cotton with a matte finish to create a soft, warm, natural look and feel.

All are available on King-Size, Snap-end Spools that contain
330 yds. of 12 wt. and 500 yds. of 30 wt.

1001 Bright White	1047 Mint Green	1225 Pastel Pink	1292 Heron Blue	1149 Deep Ecru	1077 Jade Tint
1071 Off White	1229 Lt. Putty	1115 Lt. Pink	1198 Dusty Navy	1070 Gold	0580 Mint Julep
1082 Ecru	1270 Dk. Gray Khaki	1119 Dk. Mauve	1283 Slate Gray	1128 Dk. Ecru	1046 Teal
1061 Pale Yellow	1287 French Green	1558 Tea Rose	1293 Deep Nassau Blue	1056 Med. Tawny Tan	1230 Dk. Teal
1124 Sun Yellow	1051 Christmas Green	1307 Petal Pink	1199 Admiral Navy Blue	1180 Med. Taupe	1015 Med. Peach
0567 Butterfly Gold	1232 Classic Green	1147 Christmas Red	1197 Med. Navy	1130 Dk. Brown	1304 Dewberry
1024 Goldenrod	1175 Dk. Avocado	1035 Dk. Burgundy	1031 Med. Orchid	1186 Sable Brown	1190 Med. Burgundy
1238 Orange Sunrise	1174 Dk. Pine Green	1181 Rust	1032 Med. Purple	1131 Cloister Brown	1058 Tawny Brown
1078 Tangerine	1271 Evergreen	1169 Bayberry Red	1122 Purple	1218 Silver Gray	1240 Smokey Gray
1184 Orange Red	1209 Lt. Avocado	1192 Fuchsia	1235 Deep Purple	1328 Nickel Gray	1234 Almost Black
1246 Orange Flame	1332 Deep Chartreuse	1189 Dk. Chestnut	1299 Purple Shadow	1295 Sterling	1005 Black

Endless Possibilities

Here are a few inspiring ideas for using
Sulky 12 wt. Cotton Thread. We would love to see what you
are doing with Sulky Cottons. Email your photos with
descriptions to asksulky@sulky.com.

You can Crochet by hand with Sulky
12 wt. Cotton Threads just like Joanne
Weinberg from New Bern, NC did.

Melody Robson from Lakeland, FL loved using
Sulky 12 wt. Blendables and Solid Color
Cottons for Pleating and Smocking.

Carol Ingram used Sulky 12 wt. Black Cotton to do
Wool Applique and Blanket Stitching by hand.

Sulky 12 wt. Red Cotton is ideal for Redwork by
hand or machine. No tangling like floss!

Pumpkin Market Tote

by Carol Ingram
Designer for Sulky of America

"I have always loved the subtle accents that I can add to almost every project when I use Sulky Blendables."

--- Carol

Techniques:

- Paper Piecing on **Paper Solvy**™

- 3-D Padded Leaves with Free-motion Detail

- Decorative Stitching

- Quilting and Layering

- Sturdy Handles

- Edge Stitching

- Pinked-Edge Rotary Cutting

- Enclosed Finished Seam with Bottom Corner Shaping

- Crosshatching on Base with Quilter's Guide, and more!

You'll love the convenience of the outside quilted pumpkin pocket! Finished size: approx. 17" x 13" x 4"

Materials:

- Zig-zag Sewing Machine
- Sulky Stabilizers: Fuse 'n Stitch, Tender Touch, and Paper Solvy
- Sulky Iron-On Transfer Pen – Black or Brown
- 1 piece of plain copy paper or loose-leaf paper
- Sulky 12 wt. and 30 wt. Cotton Blendables Thread #4117 Fall Holidays or #4004 Golden Flame
- Sulky 30 wt. Cotton Thread #1232 Classic Green
- Sulky Polyester Clear Invisible Thread
- Sulky 40 wt. Poly Deco Thread #1078 Tangerine
- Sulky KK 2000 Temporary Spray Adhesive
- Small Appliqué Scissors
- Rotary Cutter with pinking blade and small mat
- Tape Measure
- Chalk Marker
- Quilting Guide Bar for machine
- Quilting or Walking Foot
- Open-toe Appliqué Foot and 1/4" Foot
- 14/90 or 16/100 Topstitch Needle
- Quilter's Ruler with 45° mark
- 5" x 10" piece of foam core or plastic mesh for the bottom of the tote (optional)

Fabrics:

- 1 - 18" x 31" piece of canvas
- 1 - 3-1/2" x 36" leaf print fabric for band
- 1 - 8" x 11" leaf print fabric for inside pocket
- 1 - 8" x 11" lightweight fleece or batting (natural, off-white color)
- 1 - 3" x 44" leaf print fabric for straps
- 1 - 1-1/2" x 7" green plaid fabric for bow
- 2 - 5" x 9" pieces of green fabric for leaves
- 1 - 5" x 9" piece of lightweight batting or fleece (natural, off-white color)

Fabric Cutting Measurements for Paper-Pieced Pumpkin Pocket:

- #1 A & B - Brown Stem: 2" x 2"
- #2 & 4 A & B - Tan Background: 1-1/2" x 5"
- #3 A - Yellow Orange: 3" x 8"
- #5, 6, 7 A & B - Med. Orange: 2" x 30"
- #8, 9, 10 A & B - Light Orange: 2" x 30"
- #3 B - Dark Rusty Orange: 3" x 8"

Set up the Sewing Machine:

- Stitch Type: Decorative Feather Stitch
- Stitch Width: per chosen stitch
- Stitch Length: per chosen stitch
- Tension: Balanced
- Top Thread: Sulky 12 wt. Cotton Blendables #4117 Fall Holidays
- Bobbin Thread: Matching 30 wt. Cotton Blendables
- Feed Dogs: Up
- Presser Foot Pressure: Normal
- Presser Feet: Open-toe Appliqué or Walking Foot
- 14/90 or 16/100 Topstitch Needle
- Spool Pin: Either

Always test the settings on your machine on a scrap first. See individual settings recommended in instructions.

The pattern can be found on the CD in the back of this book.

Preparing Your Fabric:

1. **BAND:** Cut a 3-1/2" x 36" piece of leaf print fabric and fuse a 3-1/2" x 36" piece of **Sulky Tender Touch** onto the wrong side of it. Set aside.

2. **STRAPS:** Cut a 3" x 44" piece of leaf print fabric and fuse a 3" x 44" piece of **Sulky Fuse 'n Stitch** onto the wrong side of it. Set aside.

TIP: *You may need to use a muslin press cloth over the **Fuse 'n Stitch** and **Tender Touch** in case the iron is too hot. (Irons vary - better safe, than sorry!) A white paper towel or **Sulky Tear-Easy Stabilizer** will work for a press cloth in a pinch.*

Tender Touch and Fuse 'n Stitch add extra body to the fabric. When the project is complete, you'll see how nicely everything feels and behaves!

Embellishing the Background:

1. Attach the quilting guide to the machine and adjust it to 2" from the needle.

2. Using a ruler and a chalk marker, make one diagonal 45° line across the 18" x 31" piece of tote canvas. This is the first marked line for stitching the grid with the quilting guide bar on the machine. Thereafter, just follow the previously stitched line with your quilting guide.

3. With your stitch length set at about 3.0, straight stitch the first marked line, and continue stitching the 2" spaced lines across the canvas. Mark a second 45° line going the opposite direction and continue stitching the grid across the canvas.

Marking the Bag:

1. Press the canvas and lay it out lengthwise, top to bottom. Measure down 13" from the top edge and mark. Press a crease along the mark. Measure up 13" from the bottom, mark, and press a crease. Fold these two creases together and lay the tote flat. This indicates the bottom. Press the middle crease flat. You will have 3 creases – 2 bottom edges and 1 center.

Making the Paper-Pieced Pumpkin:

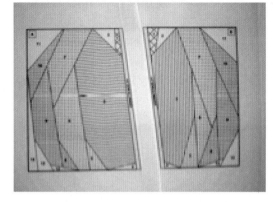

This was a barter pattern used with permission from: www.fourtwinsisters.com. Be sure to check their website for some really great quilting, paper piecing, and appliqué patterns that are available for barter. We altered it somewhat and had it re-drawn, so you won't find this exact pattern there.

1. Print the pattern, found on the CD in the back of this book, onto **Sulky Paper Solvy**.

2. Cut the **Paper Solvy** pumpkin pattern down the center on the bold line. You will be piecing the two sides of the pumpkin separately, and then sewing the centers together to finish. When stitching each #3 piece, be sure to allow for the 1/4" seam allowance on the center cut edge.

3. Thread the top and bobbin with Sulky 40 wt. Poly Deco Thread #1078 Tangerine. (Using this lightweight thread allows the seams to lay flatter.) Select a 2.0 straight stitch length.

4. Start with the first piece on the "A" side. Lightly spray Sulky KK 2000 Temporary Spray Adhesive onto the wrong side of the fabric for space #1.

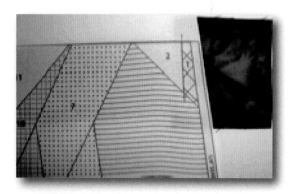

Place the fabric, right side up, on the unprinted side of the **Paper Solvy**. *(When using batiks, the right and wrong side are often irrelevant.)*

5. Flip the pattern over so the pattern is facing you and readable; stitch on the pattern along line #1.

1 & 2 stitched but not trimmed.

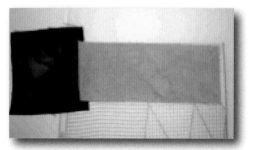

6. Spray and position the fabric for piece #2 on fabric #1 so the right sides are together, with the raw edges meeting. Flip the pattern over and stitch on the line between spaces #1 and #2. (Start 2 stitches before the line and stop 2 stitches beyond the line.) Open and finger press the seams, being gentle so you do not distort the pieces.

7. Fold the **Paper Solvy** back on itself, exposing ONLY the fabric seams. Trim the fabric seams to a 1/4" seam allowance.

Use a ruler when trimming.

8. **Remaining Piecing:** Place fabric #3, right side down, on fabric #2, with the raw edges meeting. Turn the pattern over and sew on the line between #2 and #3. Trim the seams to 1/4". Continue sewing the pieces in numerical order through #10, finishing both pattern pieces of sides A and B.

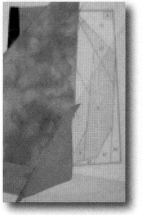

#1 through #5 stitched; fabric side.

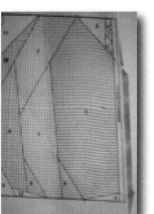

#1 through #5 stitched; pattern side.

Join the sides of the pieced Pumpkin together using a 1/4" seam allowance (as pictured above right).

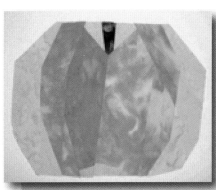

NOTE:
When doing the "pinked edge" version of the pumpkin pocket, you do not need to piece numbers 11, 12, 13, and 14. (These would be used when you wanted a finished, rectangular pocket or when you were using the pattern to make a wallhanging or quilt.)

9. When finished, tear away as much of the **Paper Solvy** as possible.

Quilting the Pumpkin:

1. Lightly spray Sulky KK 2000 on the wrong side of the 8" x 11" piece of leaf print fabric. Smooth an 8" x 11" piece of fleece or batting over the sprayed fabric. Lightly spray KK 2000 on the wrong side of the finished, pieced pumpkin and place it, right side up, on top of the batting. *Note: Carol trimmed her fleece, but it is not necessary to do so yet.*

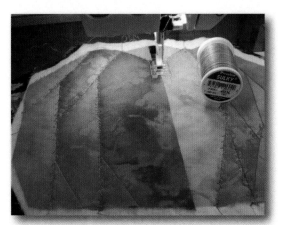

2. Attach a quilting/walking foot or open-toe appliqué foot. Thread the top with 12 wt. Blendables #4117 Fall Holidays and put a matching 30 wt. Blendables in the bobbin. Use a decorative stitch to stitch through all layers of the pumpkin sandwich along the pieced lines on the pumpkin. *The walking foot helps feed all three layers evenly.*

3. To shape the pocket, use a zig-zag or pinking rotary blade to trim around the pumpkin sandwich, through all layers.

4. Straight stitch around the pumpkin sandwich, 1/4" from the edge. Pink all the edges of your green plaid tie, and then tie a knot in the center and stitch it in place by hand or machine. You can tack the edges down with a little fabric glue to keep them positioned where you want.

Placing the Pocket:

start stitching

end stitching

1. Open the tote canvas so it lays flat. To center the pocket on it within the creased area that forms one side, measure up 2" from the bottom crease and 4-1/2" in from each side. Straight stitch 1/2" in from the edge from the upper left side of the pumpkin, down around the bottom, to the upper right side of the pumpkin, leaving the top open (which forms the pocket as indicated by the arrows). Back stitch at the beginning and end (stress points).

3-D Fabric Leaves:

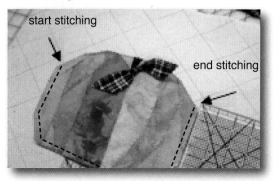

1. Use a pencil or permanent-ink marker to trace the leaf patterns (found on the CD) onto a piece of plain paper. Then, trace over these images with a Sulky Iron-On Transfer Pen. Preheat the receiving fabric with an iron. Lay the traced pattern, traced side down, on the right side of a 10" square of green fabric. Press with a dry iron to transfer the design onto the green fabric, following the directions on the pen package.

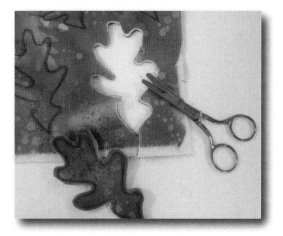

TIP: *Placing the leaf pattern on the diagonal grain (bias) will help keep the fabric from fraying.*

2. Lightly spray KK 2000 onto the wrong side of a second 10" square of green leaf fabric. Smooth a square of fleece or batting over the sprayed fabric. Lightly spray KK-2000 onto the wrong side of the first piece of green fabric that has the transferred leaves on it, and place it, right side up, on top of the batting.

3. Thread the top and bobbin with Sulky 30 wt. Cotton #1232 Classic Green, or whichever color best suits your fabric. With a 2.5 stitch length, straight stitch around each leaf just **INSIDE** the transferred lines, through all layers.

4. Use a small, sharp scissors to cut out each leaf just **OUTSIDE** the stitched lines.

5. Lay the leaves in place over the edges of the pumpkin and straight stitch down the center of each leaf, creating a center vein; add side veins as you go.

Seam the Tote:

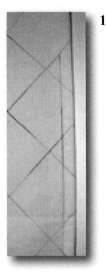

1. Lay the tote canvas out flat (18" x 31"), then fold it in half lengthwise to 15-1/2" x 18", wrong sides together. Stitch a 1/4" seam down both 15-1/2" sides. To make a totally finished seam that will not ravel (and looks clean and professional), turn the tote inside out and stitch both sides with 1/2" deep seams that enclose the 1/4" seams. Photo on the left shows the 1/2" seam partially stitched on the wrong side (inside) of the tote bag.

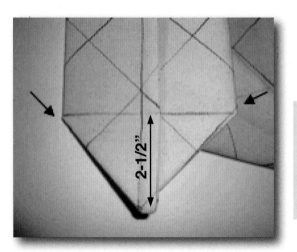

2. With the tote inside out, open it up and set it upright on its bottom. Measure 2-1/2" from the corner point, draw a straight line connecting the pressed measurements on each side, forming a triangle. Stitch across the corner on your drawn line. Repeat for the second side.

Attach the Band:

1. Press under a 1/4" hem along one long side of the prepared band. Measure the tote opening with a tape measure and add 1/4" for the seam allowances on each short end. Sew the ends of the band together using a 1/4" seam allowance to form a circle the same size as the top edge of the tote.

2. Turn the tote right side out. With raw edges matching, pin the right side of the band to the wrong side of the tote around the top of the tote; stitch it together with a 1/2" seam allowance.

TIP: *This will put the band on the inside of the bag next to the machine bed. Any slight difference in circumferences will be easier to ease-in or stretch-to-fit with the band against the feed dogs.*

3. Fold the band over towards the front and press it in place. The quarter-inch hem should still be turned under at the bottom of the band. To make the band lay well for stitching down the edge, fold the band back up, and lightly spray it with Sulky KK 2000. Smooth it back down, pin the edges and edge-stitch close to the edge of the band.

Pumpkin Market Tote

Constructing the Straps:

1. Use a rotary cutter with a pinking blade to trim one long edge of the 3" x 44" ***Fuse 'n-Stitch***-backed strap. Fold both long edges of the strap toward the center so the edges overlap and the pinked edge is on the outside. Press.

2. Put the strap under the presser foot so the pinked edge is on the underside. Use a wide decorative stitch to stitch down the center of the entire length of the strap. Cut the strap in half and pink both ends.

TIP: *Look closely at the photo on the right which shows that the pinked center edge on the wrong side of the strap is under the decorative stitching.*

3. Edge-stitch all four sides of each strap. Position the straps 3-1/2" in from each side seam (take care not to twist the strap when attaching it). Match the short, pinked edge to the bottom of the band and pin in place. Starting at the top of the band, stitch in place over the previous topstitching; backstitch substantially at the beginning and ending to reinforce the strap.

Now, proudly carry your Pumpkin Market Tote when you go shopping!

Join in the fun!

This project was featured at a recent Sulky Teacher Certification Training. If you are interested in attending one of these 3 day events to learn how to teach exciting, inventive projects like this from National Sulky Educators, in a fun, creative environment, check it out at www.sulky.com.

Sashiko Square

by Rebecca Kemp Brent - Designer

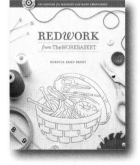

"Sulky 12 wt. Cotton Thread is perfect for machine-stitched, bobbinwork Sashiko because it is bold enough to make the pattern stand out against the dark background fabrics; and I also love the color choices. Other Sulky 12 wt. Solid Colors and even Blendables can be used for unique variations on the traditional white-on-navy-stitches."
--- Rebecca

Visit Rebecca at:
www.rkbrent.com

Materials:

- One 18" square each of: solid color cotton broadcloth, a coordinating cotton print and a flannel
- One 12" square each of Sulky® Totally Stable™ and Soft 'n Sheer™ Stabilizers
- 3" of 5/8" wide fusible web tape
- Regular Sewing Foot • 14/90 Topstitch Needle
- All purpose thread to match solid color fabric
- Sulky 12 wt. Cotton Thread in white or a light neutral color, or Blendables #4001 Parchment
- Red and Blue Sharpie®, Ultra-Fine, Permanent-Ink Markers
- The Sashiko Pattern is on the CD in the back of this book
- General Sewing Supplies

Set up the Sewing Machine:

- Thread the bobbin with Sulky 12 wt. Solid Color Cotton Thread in a neutral color, or Blendables #4001 Parchment.

- Thread the top with sewing thread to match the solid color fabric.

- Set the straight stitch length to 3.0 mm, or 8 stitches per inch.

- Sew a test line on scrap fabric; raise or lower the top tension until the bobbin thread rides on the fabric surface, with loops of the needle thread visible around the bobbin thread to define the stitches.

Construct a Grid:

1. Draw an 11" square at the center of the non-fusible surface of the 12" square of **Sulky Totally Stable Stabilizer** and mark the centers of each side.

2. Draw a grid of horizontal and vertical lines 1" apart within the square. Following the pattern shown below left, use the two colors of permanent-ink markers to draw the Sashiko pattern on the grid.

TIP: *Tape the stabilizer to a gridded cutting mat and use the mat's gridlines as a guide for drawing the Sashiko pattern.*

3. To find the horizontal and vertical center lines of the fabrics, fold them in half, then finger press them; mark with pins or 1/8" clips at each edge, then unfold them.

4. Iron the **Totally Stable** onto the flannel, matching the centerlines.

5. Stack: solid fabric (face down); then flannel and stabilizer, matching the centers. Pin the layers together. Stitch around the 11" square (the perimeter of the pattern).

TIP: *This line of stitches won't show in the finished project, so you can use it to refine stitch length and tension settings.*

A traceable version of this pattern can also be found on the CD in the back of the book, under Sashiko Patterns.

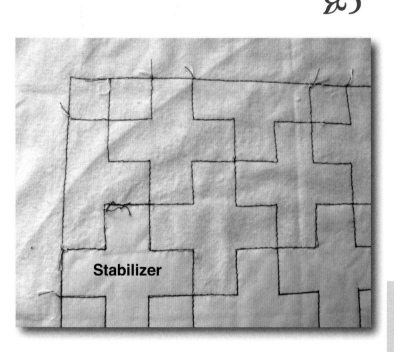

Stabilizer

6. If your machine has an automatic thread cutter, turn it off. Leave the tails of thread at each end of a line of stitches.

7. With the drawn pattern facing up, stitch the Sashiko pattern. Stitch the red lines first, then stitch the blue lines. Sew from one edge of the pattern to the other, pivoting at the corners with the needle down in the fabric.

TIP: *There should be eight stitches in each 1" segment of a line. Take a small compensating stitch, if necessary, to land the needle exactly on the pivot point.*

8. When all of the stitching is complete, pull the thread tails through to the stabilizer side of the work; knot them.

9. Carefully tear away the stabilizer. Pinch the thread knots to keep them secure as you remove the stabilizer.

10. Draw a 15-1/2" circle on pattern paper or newsprint paper (use **Sulky Soft-'n Sheer** to make a more permanent pattern), and cut it out. The edge of the pattern is the seam line for the following step.

11. Thread the top and bobbin with sewing thread. Lay the 18" square of printed fabric on the Sashiko square, with right sides together.

12. Center the circle pattern on the flannel side of the Sashiko square so the circle edge meets the corners of the square. Open the pattern and pin. Stitch the circle perimeter along the edge of the paper pattern. Remove the paper pattern and trim the seam allowances on all layers to a scant 1/4".

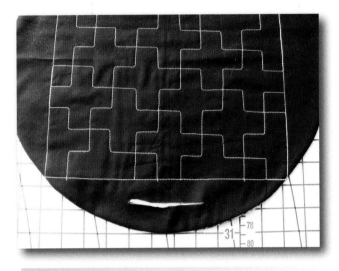

TIP: *If the allowances are trimmed to a scant 1/4" (more than 1/8" but less than 1/4"), it isn't necessary to clip or grade the curved seam. If you prefer to clip the seam allowance, use pinking shears to trim and notch the seam allowance in one step.*

13. Carefully slit only the solid fabric and flannel between the stitched square and the circle seam. Make the slit about 3" long.

14. Turn the mat, right side out, through the slit; press. Tuck the fusible web tape into the slit; arrange the cut edges to close the slit; and press to fuse.

15. With the Sashiko side on top, fold the circle edges over the Sashiko, along the stitched outline of the square. Use an appliqué stitch, blind hem stitch, or zig-zag to attach and quilt the curved edges of the circle to the Sashiko mat.

TIP: *The curved-edge stitches are shown in white for clarity; use a regular sewing thread that blends into the fabrics so your stitches are invisible.*

Sashiko Square

Team Quilt

The perfect Fund-raiser Quilt for any Team Event like Sports and Charity Walk-a-thons.

by Bev Morris - Abigayles Quiltery

Bev recommends quilting with Sulky Blendables as it adds texture and unique color change to any quilt.

"Each year our shop makes a quilt for a cancer fund-raising event in our area. The Team Quilt is a great way to honor the team spirit that makes these events successful and fun. Make one today for your favorite charity.

It is also the perfect stadium or throw-size quilt for your special sports nut.

When first designing this quilt I had my daughter, Katie, in mind. She was the pitcher for her high school softball team. See her quilt on page 26.

It's comfy for soccer Moms who spend countless hours sitting and watching.

But, it is also the perfect raffle quilt for any Team event. It just seems ideal for signing team members' or sponsors' names on the Ts to make it even more special. Use your school or event colors when choosing the fabrics for this unique quilt.

Let me know how you utilized the T-quilt; visit our shop in Olmsted Falls, OH or online: www.abigaylesquiltery.com" --- Bev

Materials:

- Sewing Machine
- 1/4" Piecing Foot with guide
- Open Quilting & Open-toe Appliqué Foot
- Size 14/90 Topstitch Needle
- Sulky KK 2000™ Temporary Spray Adhesive
- Sulky 30 wt. or 12 wt. Blendables® Thread
- Sulky Tear-Easy™ Stabilizer
- 1-1/4 yards each of 7 different background fabrics
- 3/4 yard each of 18 different dark fabrics
- 3/4 yard of binding fabric
- 6 yards of backing fabric
- 2-1/2" finished half-square Triangle Paper
- Rotary Cutter, Mat and Quilter's Ruler
- Iron and Ironing Surface
- General Sewing & Quilting Supplies

For Decorative Stitching:

- Thread the top and bobbin with a matching Sulky 30 wt. Blendables or Solid Color Cotton Thread
- Insert a 14/90 Topstitch Needle
- Attach an Open-toe Appliqué Foot
- To prevent tunneling and puckering, spray Sulky KK 2000 Temporary Spray Adhesive onto the wrong side of the fabric that you are going to embellish, and smooth 2 matching size pieces of *Sulky Tear-Easy Stabilizer* onto it
- Test and adjust tension
- Embellish as desired
- When stitching is completed, carefully tear away the *Tear-Easy,* one layer at a time

Cutting Block 1:

All strips are cut "width of fabric - W.O.F", which is about 42" to 44" wide.

Background –
- From one of the background fabrics: Cut (8) 4-1/2" strips and set them aside until final assembly
- Cut (3) 10" squares from each of the 6 remaining background fabrics, for a total of 18 squares
- Cut (3) 5-1/2" strips from each of the same 6 remaining background fabrics; from each of these strips, cut (5) 5-1/2" squares, for a total of 90 squares

Darks –
- Cut (1) 10" square from each dark fabric, for a total of 18 squares
- Cut (1) 5-1/2" strip from each of the 18 dark fabrics; from each of these strips, cut (5) 5-1/2" squares, for a total of 90 squares

Sewing Block 1:

1. Draw or press a diagonal line on the backside of the eighteen 10" background squares.

2. Layer these light background squares with the eighteen 10" dark squares, right sides together. Sew a straight seam 1/4" on either side of the drawn line. Cut apart on the drawn line. Open and press to the dark side. Line up the 45° mark on your ruler and trim these half square triangles to 8-1/2".

3. Repeat steps #1 and #2 using the 5-1/2" squares. Make 180 half squares. Trim these half-square triangles to 4-1/2".

4. Sew the 4-1/2" half squares into 2 different units, as illustrated below, keeping the same dark fabrics together in the same block. Press the seams as indicated by the arrows.

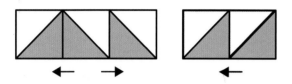

5. Assemble the blocks, adding the 8-1/2" half squares. Make (36) 12-1/2" blocks.

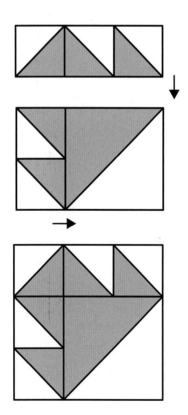

Cutting Block 2:

Background –
From each of the 6 remaining background fabrics cut (1) 7" x 17" rectangle; also cut (2) 5-1/2" squares from each fabric, for a total of (12) squares.

Darks –
Select (6) dark fabrics and cut (1) 7" x 17" rectangle from each, then cut (2) 5-1/2" squares from each, for a total of (12) squares.

Sewing Block 2:

1. Layer together pairs of light and dark rectangles, right sides together.

2. Follow the directions for the 2-1/2" triangle paper to make (120) 2-1/2" half squares. Use Sulky KK-2000 to hold these fabric sandwiches together.

3. Follow step 3 from Block 1 for the remaining 5-1/2" squares. Make (24) half squares.

4. To assemble Block 2, follow steps 4 and 5 from Block 1, using these parts. Make (24) 6-1/2" Blocks.

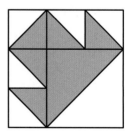

These smaller "T" blocks would be a perfect place for the team to autograph the quilt. Bring along a Pigma permanent-ink pen and portable sandpaper board (for stability). When you get home, be sure to set the ink by ironing the blocks.

Sewing the Quilt Top:

1. Piece together the 8 pre-cut background strips, end to end, into (4) long strips.

Consider commemorating your event with beautiful machine embroidered or quilted names and dates on the plain fabric strips. Another idea is to embroider or applique a photo transfer in the center of the quilt.

2. Assemble the blocks together into rows, rotating the blocks as illustrated. Sew the rows together to make the quilt top.

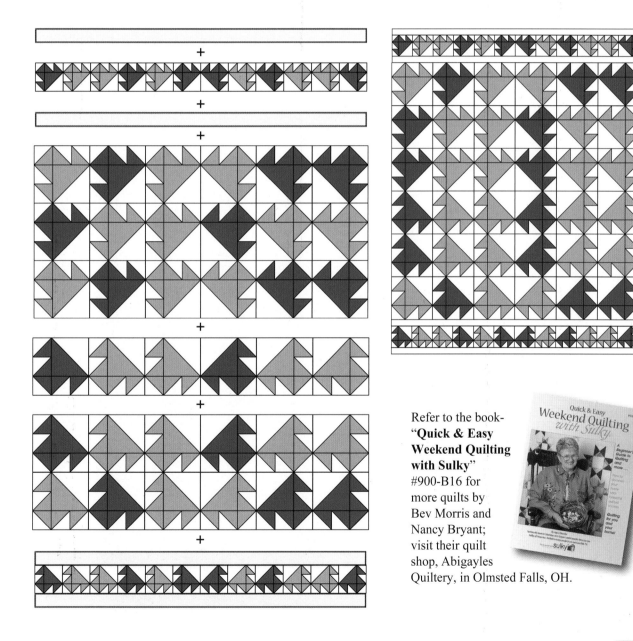

Refer to the book-
"Quick & Easy Weekend Quilting with Sulky" #900-B16 for more quilts by Bev Morris and Nancy Bryant; visit their quilt shop, Abigayles Quiltery, in Olmsted Falls, OH.

Layer the Quilt:

Batting:

There are many manufacturers and types of Batting: • Cotton • Wool • Polyester • Silk • Bamboo Blends, and they each have different qualities and loft that need to be considered for each quilting project. Quilter's Dream Cotton or Poly can be quilted up to 8" apart, and it will not shift or gravitate through the quilt top as some poor quality battings are prone to do. Ultra or High Loft battings are only suitable for tied quilts. Usually Low Loft is best for machine quilting. *(We used Warm and Natural for this project.)*

Always allow the batting to breathe and relax overnight if it has been taken out of a plastic bag where it has been tightly doubled and rolled to take up the least space in a store.

Backing Fabric:

The quilt back must be a few inches larger all around than the finished quilt top. If needed, cut and piece your backing fabric to size.

Layering the Quilt:

1. Smooth the backing fabric, right side down, onto a large surface like a quilting table or ping-pong table. To prevent shifting, secure it with either masking tape or binder clips. It should be smooth and taut, but not overly stretched.

2. Lay the batting on top of it. Smooth in place. Fold half of the batting back to expose the backing. Lightly spray the backing fabric with Sulky KK 2000. Carefully smooth the batting back into place. Repeat for the other half.

3. Place the quilt top (right side up) on top of the batting. Fold half of the top back to expose the batting. Lightly spray KK 2000 on the folded half of the quilt top. Carefully smooth the top back into place. Repeat for the other half.

4. Secure all layers of the quilt sandwich to a large, flat surface with masking tape, or use binder clips every 12" to 15".

5. On large quilts, pin every 12" in all directions using 1" brass or nickel-plated quilter's safety pins. Avoid stainless steel pins as they may rust and ruin the quilt. Remove the tape or binder clips and get ready to quilt.

Quilt It:

Thread the top and bobbin with your favorite Sulky 30 wt. or 12 wt. Cotton Thread in a solid color or Blendables color that best matches and blends with your fabrics in the quilt. If you are using 12 wt. on top, use a matching shade of 30 wt. in the bobbin. Quilt it using your favorite quilting design.

This is a closeup of the T-Quilt that Bev made in her daughter, Katie's school colors.

Sitting on it at games showed her team spirit and gave Bev a chance to talk about her love of quilting to others.

Support your Team!

Pine Scrub
at Cathedral Rock

This beautiful Southwest landscape features the thread painted Pine Scrub Tree
stitched with Sulky Blendables, Sulky Rayon and Sulky Metallic Threads.

by Chris Eichner

"The inspiration for Pine Scrub at Cathedral Rock came from viewing my many unique and wonderful photos of Arizona. I was so entranced with the illuminating skies, craggy rock formations, and Pine Scrub Tree trunks that I wanted to do a thread painting incorporating all of them.

Sulky Soft 'n Sheer Extra Stabilizer provided the perfect foundation for the multiple stitchings that were needed to eliminate puckering without adding stiffness.

Sulky 30 wt. Blendables® enhanced the intensity and subtleties of the rock formations while crafting a 3-D appearance. In order to be able to create the appliqued tree, Sulky Fabri-Solvy and Super Solvy stabilizers allowed for repeated thread applications.

The swirling effect of the bark on the trunk was easily accomplished with 30 wt. Blendables, which allowed me to create many values of color without changing spools of thread so often." --- Chris

Visit Chris at www.chriseichner.com

Materials:

Notions for Cathedral Rock:
- 1 yd. Stabilizer packages: Sulky Super Solvy, Sulky Soft 'n Sheer Extra and Sulky Fabri-Solvy
- Sulky KK 2000 Temporary Spray Adhesive
- Sulky 30 wt. Cotton Blendables® Threads: #4001 Parchment, #4011 Milk Chocolate, #4027 Silver Slate, #4033 Grape Wine, #4038 Deep Woods, #4040 Biscuit and #4044 Butterscotch
- Sulky 40 wt. Rayon Threads: #521 Nutmeg, #1080 Orchid, #1059 Dark Tawny Brown, #1111 Pastel Orchid, #1128 Dark Ecru, #1170 Light Brown, #1173 Med. Army Green, #1176 Med. Dark Avocado, #1179 Dark Taupe, #1214 Med. Chestnut, #1234 Almost Black, #1241 Dark Ash, #1272 Hedge Green, #1298 Dark Plum, #1328 Nickel Gray and #1329 Dark Nickel Gray
- Sulky Holoshimmer #6013 Fuchsia for Sky
- Sulky Clear Polyester Invisible Thread
- 1 yd. of Lite Steam-A-Seam 2™
- Free-motion/Darning Foot
- Extra-fine, permanent-ink, black Sharpie™ Marker
- Machine Needles: 14/90 Embroidery, 14/90 Metallic and 11/75 Embroidery
- Heavy Duty Spray Starch
- 6" Wooden Machine Embroidery Hoop
- Straight Pins

Fabric:
- 1 yd. of Muslin
- 1/8 yd. of each of the following Hoffman® Batiks:
  - Moss Green - *light to dark*
  - Peppered Tan - *with brown and black*
  - Dark Gray - *with terracotta*
  - Cranberry - *with gold marbling*
  - Terracotta - *with black, rust, and tan*
  - Pink - *with tan and rust*
  - Tan - *with light salmon*
  - Purple - *with pink and rust*
  - Violet - *with sage and dark pink*
  - Sky - 1/4 yd. *of light to varying shades of pink*
- 1/2 yd. of Tulle Netting - *light brown*

Plus your choice -
- 1 yd. for Backing
- 1/4 yd. for Binding
- 1/8 yd. for Border

Preparation:

1. Cut a 19" x 22" piece of muslin.

2. Cut a 14" x 17" piece of **Sulky Soft 'n Sheer Extra**; following package directions, center and fuse it onto the muslin.

3. From the CD in the back of this book, print out the patterns of the rocks and shrubs (all patterns have been reversed).

4. Spray starch and press each element fabric 3 times. To avoid white flaking, wait a few seconds each time before pressing to insure that the starch has soaked in well.

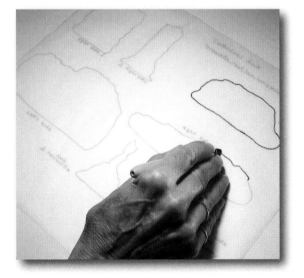

5. Cut five 10" squares of Lite Steam-A-Seam2. Remove one of the release sheets from each Steam-A-Seam cut piece (whichever one comes off the easiest). Smooth them, sticky side down, over the pattern pieces and trace them using a black, extra-fine, permanent-ink Sharpie marker.

6. Label each rock – i.e., Cathedral Rock, Butte Rock, middle, right and left rocks. Repeat for all surrounding rocks, fauna, shrubs and lighter lower rock pathway.

7. Peel and place the traced Steam-A-Seam pattern pieces onto the wrong side of the fabric which corresponds with the element descriptions and coordinating colors. Press lightly until bonding has occurred.

8. Cut out the element pieces, making sure they are labeled for correct placement.

Building the Landscape:

1. Remove the remaining release paper from each of the fused element pattern pieces as you place each one onto the muslin canvas in order, from farthest away to nearest.

2. Begin with the 6-1/2" x 17-1/2" sky fabric covering the top third of the canvas (muslin); lightly finger press in place.

3. Refer to the photos on page 27 and page 30 to help in placement of the

cathedral rock on top of the sky fabric on the right side of the canvas. Position the butte rock on the left side and center the large rock formation. Always finger press each element in place.

4. Position the next layer of rocks, working from the left side towards the middle and right side until all the rocks are in place.

5. Continue to refer to the photos to place the shrubs, fauna, trees, and the lighter fabric pathway.

Set up the Machine for Thread Painting:

- Lower the feed dogs or cover them
- Select a zig-zag stitch with a 2.5 or 3.0 width
- Lower the upper thread tension slightly
- Insert a new 14/90 embroidery needle
- Attach a free-motion/darning foot
- Thread the bobbin with Sulky Polyester Clear Invisible Thread (use for all thread painting)
- For the top, see the thread colors on the next page

Prepare the Elements:

- *Lightly press* **only the first third of the landscape** elements in place with an iron set on a medium setting.

    TIP: *You should be able to lift up the elements without too much effort in order to reposition them in case buckling occurs.*

- Pin all other elements in place.

- After you thread paint the first third of the landscape following the directions and photos on the next page, remove the pins and press the second third lightly.

Pine Scrub at Cathedral Rock

Then, thread paint the second third; remove the remaining pins, press the last third lightly, then thread paint the remaining elements.

Sulky Thread Colors Used:

For the Sky:
- Sulky 40 wt. Rayon #1080 Orchid and #1111 Pastel Orchid
- Straight Stitch with Sulky Holoshimmer #6013 Fuchsia
- Sew slowly - move the fabric slowly

For the Cathedral, Butte, and Large Center Rocks: Begin stitching with darker values followed by medium and lighter values.
- Stitch varying zig-zag widths from 2.5 to 3.0
- 30 wt. Cotton Blendables #4011 Milk Chocolate
- 40 wt. Rayon #521 Nutmeg
- 40 wt. Rayon #1128 Dark Ecru
- 40 wt. Rayon #1059 Dark Tawny Brown
- 30 wt. Cotton Blendables #4001 Parchment

For the Pink, Rust, Purple, and Lavender Rocks:
- 30 wt. Cotton Blendables #4011 Milk Chocolate for the rust and gray rocks
- 40 wt. Rayon #1214 Medium Chestnut for the rust and gray rocks
- 40 wt. Rayon #521 Nutmeg for rust and cranberry peppered fabric (*alternate straight and zig-zag stitching*)
- 30 wt. Cotton Blendables #4040 Biscuit for *straight stitching the light colored fabric middle of the landscape (follow the contours of the rock)*
- 30 wt. Cotton Blendables #4038 Deep Woods for the blue, rust and purple rocks
- 30 wt. Cotton Blendables #4033 Grape Wine for the striated fabric

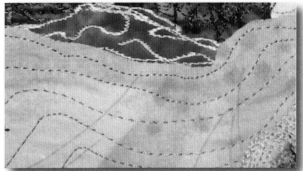

For the Upper far left side - Tree Line and Blue Area Rocks:
- 40 wt. Rayon #1298 Dark Plum

For Terracotta Rocks and Lighter Pathway Rocks:
- 40 wt. Rayon #521 Nutmeg and #1170 Light Brown
- 30 wt. Cotton Blendables #4001 Parchment and #4040 Biscuit

For the Shrubs, Trees, and Fauna:
- Select Straight Stitch

- 40 wt. Rayon #1272 Hedge Green,
  #1173 Med. Army Green and
  #1176 Med. Dark Avocado

- 40 wt. Rayon #1128 Dark Ecru
  to highlight the pine trees and grasses

- 30 wt. Cotton Blendables #4044 Butterscotch
  *for the reeds on the far left side and to highlight
  the pine trees and grasses*

Pine Scrub Tree Appliqué:

Materials:
- Cut a 12" square of Sulky Super Solvy
- Cut a 12" square of Sulky Fabri-Solvy
- Cut 2 - 12" squares of light brown or tan tulle netting
- Black, extra-fine, permanent-ink, Sharpie Marker

Tracing:

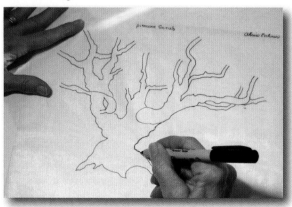

- Use the black Sharpie Marker to trace the tree design (found on the CD) onto the 12" square of **Sulky Super Solvy**

- Tightly secure the layers as follows in a 6" wooden machine embroidery hoop:

- Bottom layer - **Fabri-Solvy**

- Middle - 2 layers of Tulle Netting

- Top layer - **Super Solvy** with the traced tree

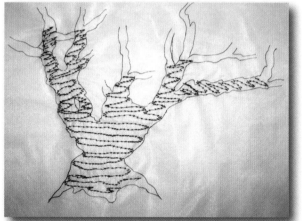

Tree Underlay Stitching:

- Form a grid with underlay stitching to strengthen the integrity of the tree trunk and main branches

- Select a 3.0 stitch width and run the machine at a medium speed as you move the hoop slowly from left to right

- Stitch within the drawn lines, leaving a 1/4" space between each row until the entire trunk and large branches have been stitched

*Begin free-motion Thread Painting the
Scrub Tree Appliqué:*
- Select Straight Stitch set at zero

- Select darker values of color first

- Refer to the picture of the finished tree to determine thread flow

- Begin at the base of the tree and stitch within the design in the hoop; if needed, re-hoop when that section has been stitched

1. Use 40 wt. Rayon #1059 Dark Tawny Brown to stitch the curved lines.

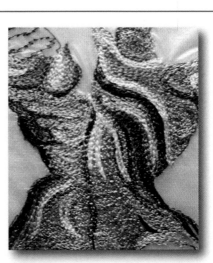

4. Add the 30 wt. Cotton Blendables #4011 Milk Chocolate and #4044 Butterscotch.

2. Use 40 wt. Rayon #1241 Dark Ash to follow the previous swirling lines and to outline the left side of the base of the tree, leaving spaces for the Cotton Blendables to be added.

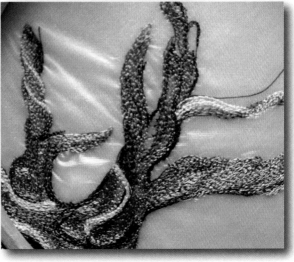

5. Add 40 wt. Rayon #1128 Dark Ecru to highlight the trunk areas and branches.

3. Use 40 wt. Rayon #1329 Dark Nickel Gray, #1328 Nickel Gray, #521 Nutmeg and #1058 Tawny Brown to continue filling in.

Follow the swirls and form new contours in the branches and in the trunk while leaving spaces to add Cotton Blendables.

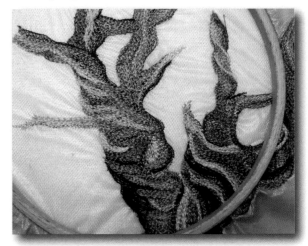

6. Add 40 wt. Rayon #1173 Med. Army Green to give the branches a mossy appearance, and in the middle of the trunk and on the large branch.

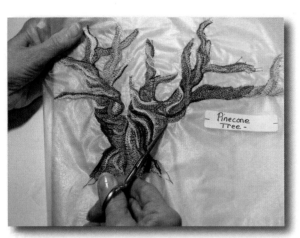

7. After you have completed thread painting the entire drawn tree, remove from the hoop.

Use a small pair of sharp scissors to cut away the stabilizers and tulle, taking care not to cut into the threads. Place a terry cloth towel on your ironing surface. Place the tree appliqué, with the right side of the stitching down, against the towel. With a steam iron at a medium setting, press lightly until the tree appliqué lies flat.

Attach the Pine Scrub Tree:

- Refer to the photo on page 27 and pin the tree applique in place
- Thread the top and bobbin with Sulky Polyester Clear Invisible Thread
- Select a 2.0 stitch width; attach the tree by sewing slowly around the outside of the appliqué with a free-motion movement

1. Cut a 12" square of **Super Solvy**; use the Sharpie Marker to draw the extending branches of the tree onto it.

2. Spray each corner of the **Super Solvy** with Sulky KK 2000 Temporary Spray Adhesive and place it over the tree appliqué, matching up the branches.

3. To create the extended branches, use a free-motion straight stitch to follow the drawn branches, starting with a darker color value.

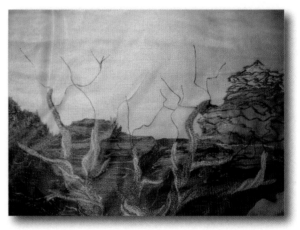

- 40 wt. Rayon #1241 Dark Ash, #1329 Dark Nickel Gray, #1058 Tawny Brown and #521 Nutmeg
- 30 wt. Cotton Blendables #4040 Biscuit and #4027 Silver Slate
- 40 wt. Rayon #1128 Dark Ecru and #1328 Nickel Gray for highlights

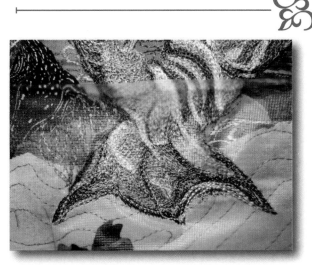

Finish the bottom of the Pine:

- Stitch the tree base with a short 2.5 zig-zag stitch before adding the grass around the base and the greenery in the foreground

- Beginning at the root base of the tree, extend the roots onto the landscape with #521 Nutmeg, #4044 Butterscotch, #1128 Dk. Ecru, and #1329 Dark Nickel Gray

Shrubs, Greenery, Reeds:

- Refer to the finished scene on page 27

- Use 40 wt. Rayon #1272 Hedge Green to free-motion straight stitch in a vertical line, curving the line to the left and right while overlapping the grasses in little groups

- Use #1176 Med. Dark Avocado to highlight the grass groups as you sparsely overlap the grass blades

- Use 30 wt. Cotton Blendables #4044 Butterscotch for the reeds. Stitch in a vertical line, veering to the left and right while overlapping the previous reeds

Borders:

Square up the finished piece:
- Trim the edges using a rotary cutter, mat and Quilter's Ruler

Add Borders & Binding:

Add a flanged, folded inner border, if desired:
- Cut strips to 1-1/2" by the width of the fabric (WOF)
- Using a 1/4" seam allowance, sew strips together to make enough to go all around the piece
- Press in half lengthwise, wrong sides together
- With right sides together, use a 1/4" seam allowance to sew the borders onto the edges of the thread painted piece

Add Outer Border:
- Cut strips to 2" by WOF
- Sew strips together to make enough to go all around the piece
- With right sides together, use a 1/4" seam allowance to sew these strips onto the raw edge of the inner border

Add Binding:
- Cut strips to 2-1/4" by WOF
- Sew strips together to make enough to go all around the piece
- Press in half lengthwise, wrong sides together
- With right sides together, use a 1/4" seam allowance to sew these strips onto the raw edges of the outer border
- Fold over to the back and hand stitch

The Perfect Cover Up

by Eric Drexler, *National Sulky Educator*

"Using Blendables thread on top and in the bobbin gave me the perfect mottled look. The 30 wt. is strong enough to be stretched over the vases, and it is thick enough to fill in large areas without a lot of extra stitches and sewing time.

Sulky Fabri-Solvy supports dense stitching perfectly.

Sometimes, I love to lightly sew over the entire piece with Sulky Holoshimmer™ Metallic Thread to give it some sparkle. Since nobody likes to see the cloudy water in the bottom of the vase, why not make a beautiful lace cover you can leave on all the time. Better yet, create one for all of the seasons or any holiday." --- Eric

Materials:

- (2) 14" squares of Sulky Fabri-Solvy™ Stabilizer
- Sulky KK 2000™ Temporary Spray Adhesive
- (1) 14" square of Tulle *(Not Organdy because it stretches)*
- 1 spool of Sulky 30 wt. Blendables Thread
- Long Quilter's Pins
- 1/4" Foot or All-purpose Foot
- Darning or Free-motion, Spring-type Foot
- Schmetz 14/90 Topstitch, Metallic, or Embroidery Needle
- Water Soluble Marker
- Spool of contrasting Thread for basting
- Wooden Embroidery Hoop - optional
- Print out the Vase Pattern found on the CD
- General Sewing Supplies

Preparation:

1. Lightly spray Sulky KK 2000 Temporary Spray Adhesive onto the right side of the vase pattern, which keeps it from shifting while tracing.

2. Center a 14" square of **Sulky Fabri-Solvy** over the pattern and smooth it in place.

3. Using a water soluble marker, trace the vase pattern onto the **Fabri-Solvy.**

4. Remove the **Fabri-Solvy** from the pattern.

5. Place the tulle on a flat surface and lightly spray KK 2000 over it.

6. Place the **Fabri-Solvy,** traced pattern side up, over the tulle and smooth it in place.

Create the Free-Motion Lace:

1. Set up the machine for free-motion:
   - Select straight stitch
   - Select needle down
   - Drop or cover the feed dogs
   - Attach a darning or free-motion, spring-type foot
   - Insert a 14/90 or 16/100 needle (for two threads through one needle)
   - Thread the top and bobbin with Sulky 30 wt. Cotton Blendables in the color of your choice
   - *Optional* - for a glitzier look, thread Sulky Holoshimmer Metallic along with the Blendables Thread in the same needle

2. To reduce puckering, sew horizontal and vertical grid lines by moving the fabric in a fluid, circular motion, forming small to medium size **circles** *that slightly overlap* for strength, but are not super filled in. You want a light, lacy effect with all circles touching each other.

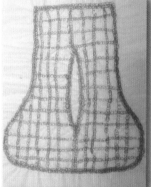

3. When filling in, start in the center of the design and work to the outside. Don't fill in the crosshatch area because it will be cut away later.

4. When stitching up to the outside design lines, stitch your circles so they cover or overlap by 3/8" to 1/2" beyond the solid drawn line. This will become your seam allowance later.

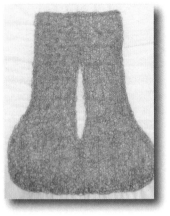

5. When all of the areas are filled with circles, check it against your pattern. Since this piece shrinks a little with wide open stitches, and a lot when filling in with dense stitches, you may have to go back and add more. Too much is okay since it will be inside the seam, but too little won't do. The last way to test for size is to wrap the stitched cover-up around the vase and pinch where the seam would be. Since glass bud vase sizes vary, hand baste your lace onto your vase and use a water soluble marker to draw revised seam lines on the *Fabri-Solvy,* leaving a 1/2" seam allowance.

6. Remove the basting and fill in any areas that may need more thread.

7. Once you are satisfied, stitch another row of circles around the outside and inside the seam lines to reinforce the edges since they will be stressed when you slide it over the vase.

Sew the Vase Cover Seam:

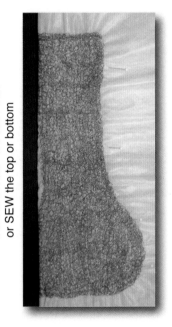

Folded in half - DO NOT PIN or SEW the top or bottom

1. **Set the Machine for a Straight Stitch:**
   - 2.0 to 2.5 stitch length
   - Raise the feed dogs and attach the all-purpose foot or 1/4" foot, if you have one
   - Continue to use the same Blendables Thread in the bobbin but change the top thread to a contrasting thread color

2. Fold the lace in half, right sides together. Line up the edges and pin them together.

3. Machine baste a 1/4" to 1/2" seam allowance from the top, outside edge, down the vase neck, and stop at the bottom. Do not sew the top or bottom closed (mark with a pin to remind yourself). To make it fit the shape of your vase, stitch the dart on the traced line. Try it on the vase again and make any necessary adjustments to make it fit your bud vase.

4. Once it fits properly, thread the top with your original Blendables color and sew all seams twice with a shorter stitch length for strength. Remove the basting stitches. Cut away the excess Tulle and stabilizer from outside the stitched lines and dart. Rinse away the *Fabri-Solvy* and turn the lace right side out. When the lace is almost dry, stretch it down over your bud vase. Dress it up with a ribbon and rose and give it to a friend or loved one. Think of the endless possibilites for things you can cover like glass candle holders and lamp shades.

The Perfect Cover Up

Shawl of Thread

Made on a Long Arm Quilting Machine

by Evelyn Byler - Long Arm Quilting Expert

Approximate
Finished Size
36" x 92"

Modeled by Britt Ammann

"The premier choice for my long arm quilting is Sulky Cotton Blendables for either a subtle coloring that blends into the background or a bold 'hey, look at me' color combination. A bit larger needle and a lower tension adjustment is all that is needed, and I am off on another creative adventure. When I just can't find that perfect solid color thread to make my project sing, especially when using batik fabrics and flannels, there is always a Blendables thread that looks custom dyed just for me."
--- Evelyn

This beautiful shawl, as seen on the front cover of the book, could also be made on a home sewing machine. The long arm approach is very much the same steps that you would take to create the shawl on a regular machine. Of course, the long arm machine has incredible speed and can handle large pieces easily.

Materials:

- Long Arm Quilting Machine
- Machine Needle - 3.5 or 4.0 Needle (110)
- 24" Quilter's Ruler
- Sharpie permanent-ink or a washout marker
- (2) 96" lengths of 20" wide Sulky Ultra Solvy Stabilizer
- (3) Spools each of Sulky 12 wt. Cotton Blendables #4051 Forever Green and #4019 Forest Floor
- (2) Spools each of Sulky 30 wt. Cotton Blendables #4019 Forest Floor and #4051 Forever Green
- (3) Spools of Sulky Sliver™ #8040 Opalescent

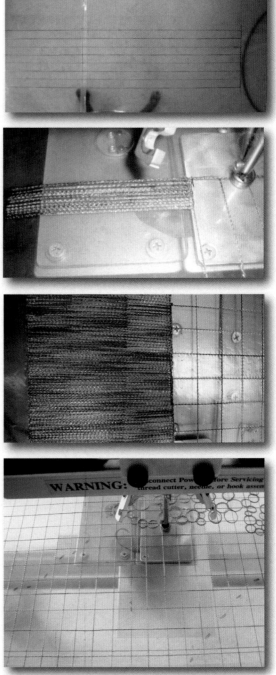

Prepare the Ultra Solvy:

1. Overlap 1/4" of the long edges of two 96" lengths of **Sulky Ultra Solvy** (cut from a 20" wide bolt); stitch them together to create one piece that is roughly 40" x 96".

2. Use a washout or permanent-ink marker to draw a 30" x 80" rectangle centered in the **Ultra Solvy** piece. At each end of the 80", mark another 4" wide area for fringe. Write "fringe" in this area to remind you not to stitch a grid into it.

Grid and Fringe Construction:

1. Thread the top with Sulky 12 wt. Blendables #4051 Forever Green and put a matching 30 wt. #4051 in the bobbin. Mount the **Ultra Solvy** on the machine with the SHORT SIDES to the leaders, the way you normally mount a quilt back.

2. Starting on the left and right sides, make a mark for the first five grid lines each 3/4" apart.

3. Begin at either corner and stitch straight across the 30" width of the rectangle. At the opposite side, stitch down 3/4"; then straight back to the beginning side; then down 3/4"; and straight back to the second side. Continue like this until the entire 80" length inside the marked fringe area is covered with back and forth stitching lines, 3/4" apart.

4. If your machine has a stitch regulator, count the number of stitches it takes to stitch that 3/4". Determine a good average and you won't have to measure and mark anymore. For this project, counting the stitches down for each turn is close enough.

5. If your machine has a channel lock option, it will help keep the grid lines straight. As a bobbin runs out, replace it and stitch again over the previous inch. Later, add circles at these spots to make the ends secure.

6. Remove the *Ultra Solvy*, turn it, and remount it to the leaders on the frame so the shawl will be lengthwise. Begin again at a corner, stitching straight out into the fringe area; then across and into the fringe area on the opposite side; down 3/4"; and back again as before. Stitch and fill in as you go, one 3/4" segment at a time. Stitch each fringe as close to the next as possible without crossing. The stitching on the grid side MUST cross the first perpendicular grid thread line. Any portion not crossing over a previous line of stitching won't be held together when the *Ultra Solvy* is washed out. Proceed across the width and down the length of the shawl until the 30" x 80" rectangle is gridded with 3/4" spaced squares, with a fringe on each side.

Make the Circles:

1. Use a marker to draw an outline of where you want the colored areas to be. Evelyn used a swoosh through the middle without changing thread colors. To add a subtle color change for the outside margins, she changed the bobbin thread to 30 wt. #4019 Forest Floor and left spaces between the margins and the swoosh. She changed the top thread to 12 wt. #4019 to stitch the remaining areas.

2. To emulate this design, begin at the edges of the shawl and stitch in circles, going around each one 2-3 times; make differing sizes next to, and just overlapping each other. Fill in each area of designated color with circles, leaving a few, small, negative spaces showing only the thread grid. Keep the distribution of circles even throughout, but cover the edges a bit more for stability.

3. When all of the circles are finished, thread the top and bottom with Sulky Sliver Metallic #8040 Opalescent. Since Sliver is a flat thread, it must be pulled from the SIDE of the spool to avoid breakage. If you do not have a spool pin or adapter that will allow the thread to feed from the SIDE of the spool, for a temporary solution try taping a crochet hook in the line of the normal thread path, prior to the tension assembly. If you normally spiral thread through a flat guide, rethread to go in the first hole and straight out the third hole. Create metallic circles in the negative spaces where only the thread grid is present. Travel along the Blendables' circles from area to area rather than tying off repeatedly.

Remove the Ultra Solvy:

1. Remove the shawl from the frame and trim off unstitched areas of the *Ultra Solvy*. Soak the shawl in luke-warm water, and gently move it back and forth. After several minutes, change the water and continue to soak and gently agitate until the shawl does not feel sticky. Gently squeeze, but do not twist, to remove most of the water. Lay flat to dry.

Key Keeper

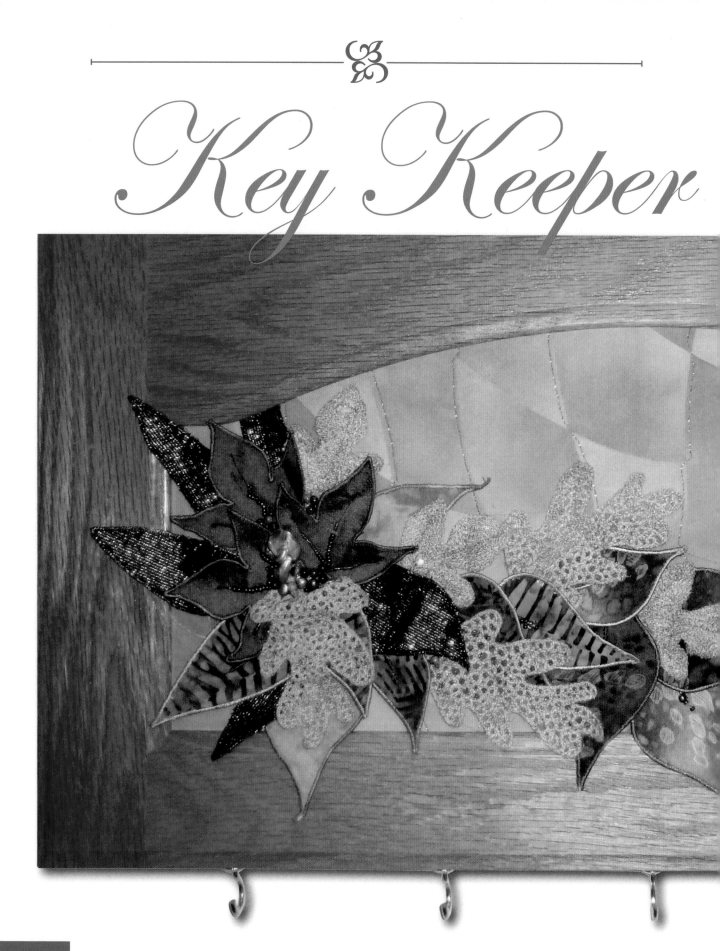

Key Keeper Leaves

Leaves

by Evelyn Byler

"The décor in the room for which this key keeper was made is perfectly expressed in the colors of the Sulky Blendables thread #4024 Heather. All of the fabrics and coordinating threads used are anchored by the soft greens and purples contained in this thread.

More fabrics and threads are added that match the colors of the original #4024 color palette. Then, a few darker values are added, as well as some to the warm or pink side of the purples and the cool or blue side of the greens. The colors for the threads used for satin stitching are chosen to emphasize a color or to add contrast.

The different leaf construction techniques are organized by the stabilizers used to make them."
--- Evelyn

This "**Bonus Project**" can be found on the CD in the back of this book.

Bouclé Lace Purse

Making Fabric from Sulky Blendables Cotton Thread

by Jim Suzio - Designer

Modeled by Tess Love

"Creating your own original project is always exciting, but when that also includes making the fabric to create the project, it's even more so. This purse project is truly unique and one-of-a-kind, and it is reversible when using a different color thread on top and in the bobbin. This creates a tweed effect. The purse features a shoulder length strap that can be made shorter or longer as you require. Or, for more versatility, you can omit the strap completely and make it as a clutch purse (great as a wedding attendant's gift for the bridal party!)." --- Jim

The purse can be made manually using free-motion techniques, or Jim offers it as an in-the-hoop, digitized design for computer embroidery on his website: www.jimsuzio.com

Instructions for this **"Bonus Project"** are on the CD in the back of this book.

Cosmetic Bag
or Serger Change Purse

by Ellen Osten - Director of Education for Sulky of America

Finished size 8" x 8".

A Sulky 12 wt. Blendables and a coordinating solid color were the perfect combination!

Back View

Materials:

- Three-Thread Serger and a Zig-zag Sewing Machine
- 2 spools of your favorite color of Sulky 12 wt. Cotton Blendables® and 2 spools of a complementary solid color of 12 wt. Cotton
- 4 - 250 yd. spools of Sulky 40 wt. Poly Deco™ to match the 12 wt. solid color Cotton and Blendables
- 24 - 1" x 12" pieces of Sulky Cut-Away Plus™ Stabilizer (this longer size is easier to handle)
- 1 - 8-1/2" square of Sulky Tender Touch • 3 - 8-1/2" squares of Sulky Soft 'n Sheer Extra Stabilizer
- 1 - 8-1/2" square of Sulky Fuse 'n Stitch™ Stabilizer • 4 - 8-1/2" squares of med. wt. Cotton Fabric
- 2 - 9" Zippers with plastic teeth (no metal) • Zipper Foot • Double-Sided Basting Tape
- Rotary Cutter, Mat and Ruler • Glass head pins • Press Cloth • Point Turner
- Chalk Marker • Tiger Tape or Masking Tape • General Sewing Supplies

Set up the Serger:

- Use a 3-thread Serger

- Wide overlock • Left needle only

- Thread the same color of Sulky 40 wt. Poly Deco in the left needle

- Thread the Sulky 12 wt. Cotton Blendables in the upper and lower looper

- Suggested Stitch length - 1 mm

- Adjust tensions to obtain a balanced stitch

Construction:

1. Serge along one long edge of a 1" x 12" strip of *Sulky Cut-Away Plus* stabilizer. As you serge, trim a bit of the stabilizer, which will help form an even stitch.

2. Turn the strip around (still right side up) and serge down the other long edge, with the left needle just touching the edge of the previous stitching. Repeat this process on 11 more strips.

3. Change the thread in the upper and lower looper to the 12 wt. solid color cotton thread and repeat with the other 12 strips.

4. Place the 8-1/2" square of *Sulky Fuse 'n Stitch*, fusible side up, on a pressing surface. With the right sides up, center 12 strips of the same color, side by side **vertically**, on top of the *Fuse- 'n Stitch.*

5. Lift up every other row as you weave each of the 12 other color strips in place, until the *Fuse 'n- Stitch* is covered. Use glass head pins on the outside edge of the strips to hold them in place as you weave. Be sure they are snug together with no gaps.

6. Cover with a pressing cloth. Use steam to press strips onto the *Fuse 'n Stitch*. Put Tiger Tape or Masking Tape along the edge. Remove the pins. To complete the fusing process, turn the piece over and press again.

7. Use a ruler and chalk marker to mark the 4 sides to measure 8-1/2" square. To even up all 4 sides, use a rotary cutter and ruler to cut on the drawn lines. Thread the top and bobbin of your sewing machine with the Poly Deco Thread. With the *Fuse 'n Stitch* side up, straight stitch (stay stitch) along the edge on all four sides, just inside a 1/4" seam allowance; then edge stitch or serge all four sides.

Note: If using a serger, you can cut and serge all the edges at the same time.

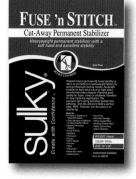

Blendables overlocked over Sulky Cut-Away Plus Stabilizer

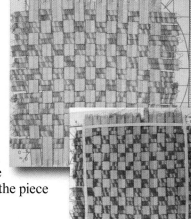

Cosmetic Bag or Serger Change Purse

8. Place double-sided basting tape on the right side edge of the zipper. Lay the right side of a 9" zipper tape on the ***right side*** of the 8-1/2" woven square, with the ends of the zipper extending beyond the sides. Use a zipper foot to sew the zipper in place.

Prep the Bag Back, Lining and Outside Pocket:

1. On the wrong side of the Bag's back fabric, press ***Sulky Soft 'n Sheer Extra***. Back the Lining Fabric with ***Soft 'n Sheer Extra***. Back the Pocket with ***Sulky Tender Touch***. Fold the pocket in half with the wrong sides together.

2. Place double-sided basting tape on the fold

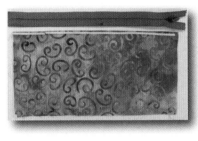

of the pocket fabric. Remove the release paper and stick it onto the right side of the zipper tape edge.

3. Use a zipper foot to sew the zipper.

4. Lay another 8-1/2" square of fabric (for the

back of the bag), right side up, on a flat surface. Position the zipper pocket on top, matching the three cut edges.

Topstitch the unsewn side of the zipper tape.

5. Sew the single edge of the back fabric to the zipper tape that is opposite the side sewn to the serged piece in #8 above. Double check

that the front and back match, and that the pocket/zipper opening is going to open in the correct position.

Bag Construction and Lining:

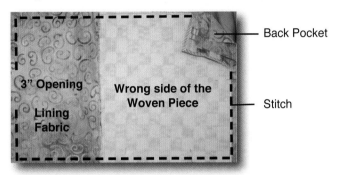

1. Sew the right side of one of the two remaining fabric pieces to the wrong side of the zipper tape on each side, just inside the previous stitching line.

2. **Open both zippers**. Machine bartack or use a small piece of tape to hold the zipper tape/teeth together when you sew the lining and bag front to the lining and bag back, right sides together. Leave a 3" opening on one side of the lining for turning. Clip the corners and cut off the ends of the zipper tape. Reinforce the ends of the zipper tapes with bartacks.

3. **Turn right side out.** Close the opening in the lining. Tuck the lining into the bag. Use a point turner to poke the corners out. Lightly press if needed.

Serger Crochet

A Sulky Blendables® Thread Doily

by
Joan Friedrich
Author,
Babylock Educator

"Sulky Solid Color Cottons and Blendables threads are great to use with the serger crochet technique. They lay nicely with the loops and make the serger crochet look like it was made by hand. The crochet washes nicely and holds its shape. The solid colors are rich-looking and the Blendables come in so many beautiful color combinations." --- Joan

More ideas for using beautiful Sulky Blendables Serger Crochet Lace, (like this Onesy by Ellen Osten) are in the Gallery on the CD in the back of the book.

Look for Joan's book, **Serger Crochet, with Nancy Zieman,** that is filled with many beautiful projects.

Materials:

- Serger with 4 threads capability and a clear foot
- 14/90 Needle
- 3 spools of your favorite Sulky 12 wt. Blendables® Thread
- 1 - 4" x 12" strip of Sulky Cut-Away Plus™ Stabilizer
- 1 - 9" square of Cotton or Linen fabric
- Double-eyed hand needle • Extra-fine, Permanent-Ink, Sharpie® Marker
- Seam Sealant • Spray Starch • Paper Clips
- Rotary Circle Cutter and Mat or a circle compass

Create the Linen Center:

1. Press and heavily spray starch the 9" square of cotton or linen. Find the center by folding it in half, then in half again; finger press along the creases.

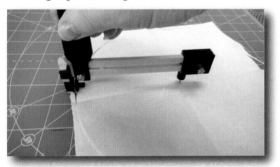

2. Open the 9" square and cut an 8-1/2" circle from it. A rotary circle cutter works well, otherwise use a compass and mark a line to cut.

Set up the Serger:

- Insert a 14/90 needle in the left needle position.
- Set the stitch length on the longest stitch (such as 4 or the longest that your machine will make).

- Set the stitch width to the widest setting, which will remain the same throughout the project.
- Attach the clear foot on the serger.
- Thread your serger with 3 spools of your favorite color of Sulky 12 wt. Blendables Thread.
- Engage the cutting blade so that it will cut on the first round.
- Use an extra-fine, permanent-ink Sharpie marker to place a dot on your serger between the left needle position and the right needle position (this is where you are going to guide the rows of loops so the next row will fall in the center of the last row).
- (To remove the dot after you finish the project, use an alcohol swab, or check with your dealer to see what they recommend for your machine.)

Begin Stitching:

1. Place the edge of the 8-1/2" circle of linen or cotton under the foot. To get an even edging as you serge around the circle, you may need to lift up the presser foot to readjust it.

2. Before stitching on the fabric, serge about a 3" tail as a marker for the beginning and ending of your rows.

3. Serge around the circle one time and, as you get back to the beginning and see the thread tail, move it to the left of the machine; do not cut it off. This is your counting reference. Each time you go around, stop at this point and count each row as you go. Now, disengage the serger blade.

4. The foot has been removed in the next photo only so that you can see that the first row of stitching is finished.

5. Move over to the middle of the first row and stitch around the circle again.

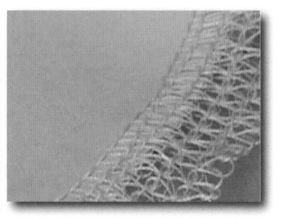

6. As you continue around each row, slightly move over to the right of the previously stitched row.

7. You will be adding stitches on top of stitches. Make about 8 rows with the stitch length at 4.0 and stop at the beginning point.

Begin to Ruffle:

1. Adjust your stitch length 1/2 of a step lower (go to 3.5 if you were at 4.0) and stitch 3 more rows; then adjust your length to 3.0. Make several rows at this length and you will begin to see it getting fullness in the ruffle.

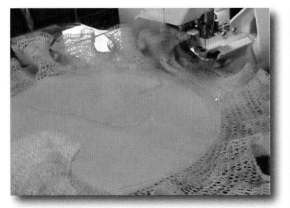

2. Continue stitching 3 rows around the doily at 2.5, 2.0 and 1.5. At the 1.0 setting, only apply 1 row, which is your last row of stitching. With a double-eyed needle, run the thread tail back through some of the stitching.

2. Use paper clips to hold it together, then start to pin the ruffles to it.

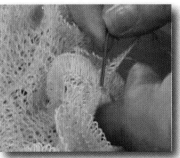

3. Clip the thread tail and apply a seam sealant to the ends.

...hen you are finished pinning, lightly spray the ruffles with a spray starch several times, letting it dry in between each application. When the doily is dry, remove the pins, clips and the Cut-Away Plus, and enjoy your beautiful ruffled doily.

Tip: If you miss a stitch, you can easily go back with the same thread and a needle, and whip stitch it together.

If you make more or less rows, that's okay, your doily may be fuller or not as full.

Experiment and have fun.

Make a Circular Collar

1. Let's put on the finishing touch. To make a collar to go in the center of the doily, measure the circumference of the fabric of the doily and cut a slightly larger piece of **Sulky Cut-Away Plus** Stabilizer that is about 4" wide.

Squared-to-be-Hip Reversible Belt

by Pam Laba - Designer

"Ahh, Fabulous Sulky Blendables! They were the perfect thread for this belt because their weight, texture, and multi-colors that changed often and randomly added just the right pop to make the belt stand out. Have fun making this unique belt on your Serger!" --- Pam

Instructions for this **"Bonus Project"** are on the CD in the back of this book.

Serger Coaster Wraps

by June Garris

"I love the way the Sulky Blendables® look on a serged edge.
They add so much interest and subtle color changes that impact the look and
quality of the finished coaster. Enjoy making these when you need a quick gift
for your favorite hostess or a shower gift. Everyone loves receiving these." --- June

Materials:

- Zig-zag Sewing Machine and Serger

- 14/90 Needle for the serger; 16/100 Jeans, Topstitch or Embroidery Needle for the sewing machine

- Open-toe Appliqué Foot

- Wooden Skewer, Tweezer or Stylus

- A Wooden, Spring-type Clothespin

- Sharp, Pointed Scissors

- 24" Quilter's Ruler

- Rotary Cutter and Mat

- 3 spools or cones of Sulky 30 wt. Cotton Blendables® Thread that complements your chosen fabric

- Sulky KK 2000 Temporary Spray Adhesive

Various Light and Dark Fabrics:
- For the 6 - 5" Coasters:
  Cut 5 - 3/4" x 22" strips of each of 3 dark and 2 light colors

- For the Coaster Bowl:
  Cut 8 - 3/4" x 22" strips of each of 3 dark and 2 light colors

- For the Bows on the Coaster Bowl:
  2 - 1" x 22" strips with a rolled hem on **both sides** of the strips

Clothesline:
- Approximately 66 inches for each Coaster
- 20 feet per Coaster Bowl

Set up your Serger for a rolled hem according to your owner's manual:

- Insert a 14/90 needle in the right needle position

- Thread the loopers and right needle with Sulky 30 wt. Blendables Thread

- Remove the left needle

- Select a rolled hem setting

- Test and adjust

Roll Hem the Fabric Strips:

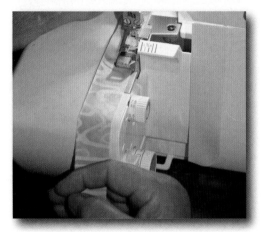

1. Continuously feed all of the fabric strips under the serger's foot, making a sewn edge on one side only.

2. Cut the strips apart from one another.

3. Sort them by colors (if using different colors) and band them together for easy access.

Set up your Sewing Machine:

- Attach an open-toe appliqué foot
- Insert a 16/100 topstitch needle
- Thread the top and bobbin with the same color of Sulky 30 wt. Blendables that matches the fabric
- Select a multiple zig-zag stitch (3 or 4 step zig-zag stitch)
- Set width to 2 mm
- Select a medium length or 12 to 13 stitches per inch
- Select the needle down feature, if available

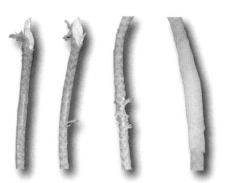

TIP: Aways trim the end of the cord; taper it when ending the project; use *Soft 'n Sheer Extra* as a band-aid to join two cord ends.

The Basics of Wrapping the Clothesline:

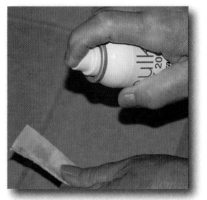

1. Set up a box for spraying and spray Sulky KK 2000 Temporary Spray Adhesive on the wrong side of one end of a fabric strip.

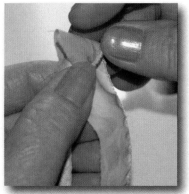

2. Hold the serged end to the right and fold about 3/4" of the end, wrong side down, at a 45° angle over the trimmed, raw edge of the clothesline.

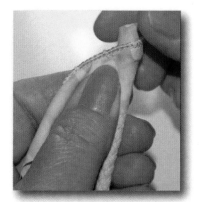

3. Start wrapping the fabric strip on a diagonal around the clothesline, with each wrap overlapping the previous one so that no clothesline shows.

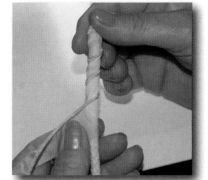

4. Wrap about a foot at a time and secure the end with a clothespin.

Begin to Coil the Wrapped Clothesline:

1. Tightly coil the wrapped clothesline onto itself and stitch an "X" over it.

2. Keep coiling and stitching until you approach the clothespin.

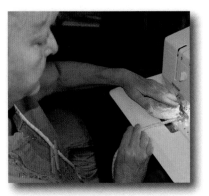

3. Keep the stitched clothesline to the left so the coil is always flowing clockwise to the outside of the machine.

4. Keep the wrapped clothesline centered under the presser foot so that the multiple zig-zag stitch catches the sides of both coils. While sewing slowly, continue by simply snugging the wrapped cords against one another with a stylus or bamboo skewer; make sure the serged edge always shows.

5. Set your machine for needle down (if your machine has that feature), or turn your hand wheel towards you and stop with the needle down when you notice the clothespin getting close.

6. To change colors or add a strip, spray both sides of the new strip with KK 2000 to help hold it together with the existing strip and the cord. Begin wrapping it over the first fabric strip, in the same spiral-wrapped direction, so that none of the clothesline is visible.

7. Put a clothespin on it to hold it in place, and continue stitching.

The Final Wrap:

1. To end, cut the clothesline at an angle. Cut the fabric 1" longer.

2. Spray the end of the fabric strip with KK 2000.

3. Wrap the fabric strip around the cut end. Fold the 1" of remaining fabric to the INSIDE of the end; tuck it under and sew it into the last fabric-wrapped row.

Coaster's Bowl:

1. Make a 5" coaster as the bottom of the bowl. To begin making the sides of the bowl, start tilting the next row up toward the machine. Continue until the bowl is the size you want. Refer to the photo on page 53.

2. When sewing the last round of cord, leave enough wrapped cord unattached to make a handle.

3. Secure the cord to the top and second round. Take the remaining cord you saved for the handle and sew across it to secure the wrap.

4. Make 2 bows from the 2 - 1" x 22" fabric strips that are roll-hemmed on both sides. Tie them to both sides of the handle as shown on page 53.

Serger Wraps

by Eric Drexler - Sulky National Educator

"I have always loved making corded bowls but wanted a way to clean up the scrappy raw edge. The first experiments were with contrasting colors. Wow did the edges ever show up! Not only did they beam with color, but the random color change actually gave it a spiraling effect when it was finished. I loved it, loved it, loved it."
--- Eric

Instructions for this **"Bonus Project"** are on the CD in the back of this book.

Do you Knit?

Make your own unique yarn with Sulky 12 wt. Cotton Blendables Thread and your Serger's Overlock Stitch.

With 126 colors to choose from, your hardest decision will be what color to use.

Carol Ingram used 3 spools of Sulky 12 wt. Cotton Blendables #4016 Peacock Plume to make a serger chain of overlock, which she then knitted into this lovely Drop-Stitch Scarf.

Drop-Stitch Scarf

1. Use a Size 9 Circular Needle or straight needles.

2. Loosely cast on 24 stitches.

3. Knit 10 rows (5 ribs) back and forth.

4. Knit next row with a double wrap (wrapped twice around the working needle).

5. Knit the next row, dropping the extra loop as you knit; knit 9 more rows (5 ribs).

6. Repeat this pattern until you reach the desired length.

7. End with 10 knit rows (5 ribs).

8. Bind off.

My Heart

Hand Embroidery on Paper with Sulky 12 wt. Blendables

by Patti Lee

Sulky Vice President of
Consumer Relations

The Sticky Note Holder
"Bonus Project"
Instructions can be found
on the CD in the back of this book.

*"I love making the heart. You will find that it takes almost no concentration and it is
finished very quickly. The Sulky Blendables keep it interesting with their
constantly and randomly changing colors." --- Patti*

Daisy Chain

"Thread Sketching" with Sulky® 30 wt. Cotton Blendables® Thread in combination with Tsukineko™ All-Purpose Inks. Inking instructions are on the CD in the back of this book.

Let Linda Visnaw take you on a creative journey where you will see how to transform free-motion or computer-embroidered, "thread sketched" designs into quilted art. This simple Daisy Chain Placemat and Napkin Set will be your first stepping stone to other fabulous creations.

by Linda Visnaw

Linda is a Certified Quilting Instructor, a Certified Golden Threads Instructor, and a Sulky Thread Artist. She holds a BA in Art Education and a Masters in Adult and Community Education. She is a National Viking Educator.

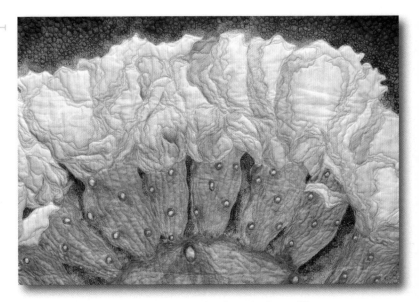

"Desert Wonder" Quilted, Inked Wallhanging

"Very simply and very dramatically, Sulky Blendables Thread brings my quilts to life. It adds texture, movement, and depth. The huge variety of colors makes it easy to find just the right combination to flow naturally through the quilted design and bring it to life.

When you Thread Sketch, you are tracing the design with your sewing machine's needle and thread. You have already traced the design on the fabric with a marker and now you will stitch over the lines with thread. When someone sketches on paper, they make a variety of lines, and then the brain chooses the right line. There is a type of drawing called Contour Drawing in which the pencil never leaves the surface of the paper. The pencil travels over the paper, defining the image by using many lines next to each other. This exact same process is used while Thread Sketching; you follow the lines you have traced and then stitch over the area several times, bringing the object to life. The brain chooses the correct line.

Thread Sketching is a perfect warm-up and great practice for becoming more comfortable, and eventually proficient, with other free-motion techniques. You need to become comfortable with controlling the movement of the fabric along with the speed of the machine before you can easily and confidently free-motion stipple, or create stars, swirls, hearts or flowers. This type of free-motion is perfect for background quilting and it is your personal preference as to whether you add a background. Take your time and enjoy your new-found proficiency, and the great Art you can create." --- Linda

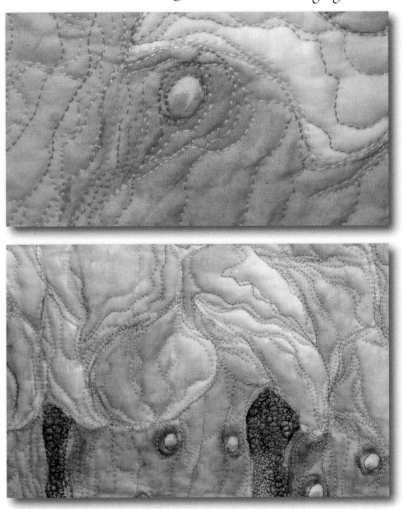

Above are pictures of "Desert Wonder" by Linda. For inspiration and/or to inquire about having her teach in your area, visit her website: www.lindavisnaw.com

Materials:

Supplies needed to Ink-Color the Daisy Chain Placemat and Napkin:

- Daisy Chain Thread Sketched Design Pattern - found on the CD in the back of this book

- Fabrico™ Dual Head Markers: Celadon, Heritage Pine, Sand, Apricot and Lemon Yellow

- Tsukineko® Inks: Celadon, Lemon Yellow and Wisteria - Available on-line: www.havasuquilts.com

- Aloe Vera Gel skin lotion - Available at your local drug store

- Various sizes of Watercolor "stroke" type brushes with angled bristles that are stiff

- White Paper Towels • Plastic Table Cover

- Q-Tips™ • 3 Small Jars

- Plastic Paint Pallet (release sheets from stabilizers like Sulky Sticky Fabri-Solvy work well also)

- Teaspoon and Ink Droppers • Gloves like Machingers™

- Iron, Ironing Pad • Teflon Sheet like Sew Slip™

- Painter's Removable Masking Tape • Light Table

- *Optional* - Swarovski 2mm/3mm Crystal AB stones and Setter

Fabric:

- Prepared for dying fabric - PFD - or wash your fabric choice before using --- no fabric softener added. Fabric can be 100% cotton, linen or silk. Use a light colored fabric for easy tracing.

Supplies Needed to Thread Sketch the Placemat and Napkin:

- Free-motion, Spring-type Darning or Open-Toe Quilting Foot

- 14/90 Topstitch or Embroidery Needle

- Sulky 30 wt. Cotton Blendables® Threads: #4057 Fresh Butter, #4003 Sunset, #4017 Lime Sherbet, and #4019 Forest Floor

- Sulky 60 wt. PolyLite™ Thread #5005 Lilac Field

- Sulky KK 2000™ Temporary Spray Adhesive

- Sulky Sticky Fabri-Solvy™ Stabilizer

- Non-Stick, Free-Motion Supreme Slider™

Basic inking instructions are found on the CD in the back of this book. Follow these instructions to complete the inking portion of this project. Visit http://www.sulky.com/books/900B21/daisychain.phpx. and watch the How-to Videos - "Inking with Linda Visnaw" and "Thread Sketching".

Whether "Thread Sketch" patterns are used for quilting, garment embellishment, or home decorating projects, the following tips and techniques will help you as you begin creating beautiful things with threads and inks together! You can also utilize the digitized, outlined embroidery designs found at www.sulkyembclub.com.

Prepare the Napkin Fabric:

1. After you have ink-colored the napkin and placemat fabric (following Linda's directions on the CD in the back of this book), cut a piece of ***Sulky Sticky Fabri-Solvy*** Stabilizer large enough to cover the Daisy design area and extend past it about an inch all around.

2. Peel away the release sheet and adhere the ***Sticky Fabri-Solvy*** to the back of the colored design on the napkin.

3. Set up your machine for Free-motion:

- Attach a spring-type, free-motion darning or open-toe quilting foot.

- Drop or cover the feed dogs.

- Insert a 14/90 embroidery or topstitch needle.

- Thread the top with Sulky 30 wt. Blendables #4057 Fresh Butter.

- Wind the bobbin with Sulky 60 wt. PolyLite Thread #5005 Lilac Field.

- Install a straight stitch needle plate, if available.

- Select the straight stitch setting - 0 length, 0 width.

- Adjust the tension for a balanced stitch.

- Select a medium to slow speed setting and needle-down position.

- Position a non-stick, free-motion, Supreme Slider under the needle to eliminate drag.

Thread Sketch the Daisy:

1. Place the stabilized, ink-colored napkin under the needle and lower the presser bar. The Daisy will be stitched first.

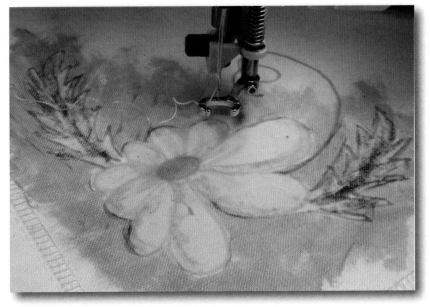

2. To begin stitching at the center of the Daisy, hold the needle thread and turn the hand wheel until the bobbin thread is brought to the top of the fabric.

3. To tie on the thread and keep it from unraveling, hold both threads and stitch a couple of stitches in place before clipping the thread tails.

NOTE: *If your machine speed is set to 1/2, push the pedal all the way down and leave it there. Move the fabric at your own comfortable speed. Forget about your foot control and only concentrate on the movement of the fabric. The stitch length is determined by how fast you move the fabric.*

To make a big difference in your ease of stitching, use a single-hole needle plate and a spring-action darning or open quilting foot that comes down and holds the fabric each time the needle goes into it. For detailed free-motion instructions, refer to the book, **"Sulky Secrets to Successful Embroidery"** ***900-B15.***

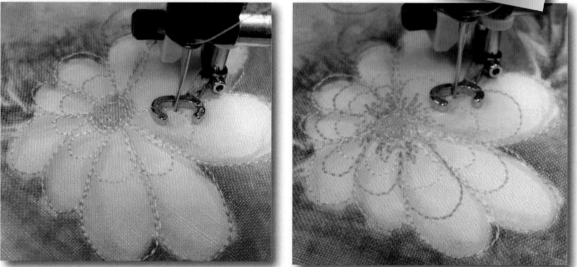

4. Stitch-trace the colored center of the Daisy in a spiral motion, finishing on the outer edge of the center. Do not try to follow the lines exactly. This is what makes it "Thread Sketching". The quickly changing colors in the Blendables Thread make the depth and tone of the design come alive.

5. Stitch around the Daisy Petals two times. One row of stitching should be to the outside and one closer to the center.

6. To finish, make a few stitches in place to tie-off. Pull the fabric towards the back of the machine and clip the top and bobbin threads, leaving a bobbin tail.

7. Thread the top with Sulky 30 wt. Blendables #4003 Sunset. Bring up the bobbin thread, hold both thread tails, and tie-on. Stitch around the petals, passing between the two yellow rows of stitching. Tie-off.

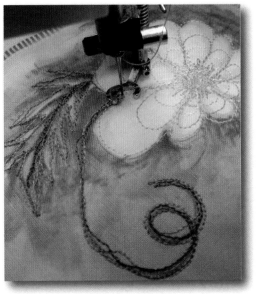

Daisy Leaves and Tendril:

1. Thread the top with 30 wt. Blendables #4017 Lime Sherbet. Bring up the bobbin thread, hold both thread tails, and tie-on.

2. Stitch up the vein and around each leaf and tendril one time. *Do not try to follow these lines exactly. If the lines are spiky and wavy, that is the look you want.*

3. Repeat with the 30 wt. Blendables #4019 Forest Floor on top.

Finishing Up:

1. Pull the excess **Sticky Fabri-Solvy** away from the stitching and run a wet Q-Tip over the outer stitching lines; the excess **Sticky Fabri-Solvy** should come away easily. Follow the package directions for removing the remaining **Sticky Fabri-Solvy.**

2. Press it and set it aside to pair with one of the placemats you will make next.

Daisy Chain Placemat:

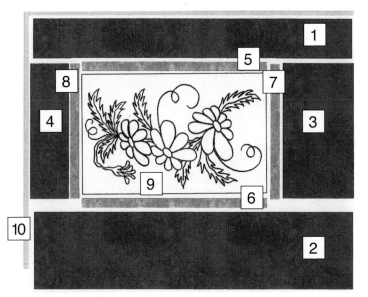

Fabric Key (1 Placemat):
- From 3/8 yd. of Purple:
  #4 - Cut (1) - 2-1/2" x 7-1/2" piece
  #1 - Cut (1) - 2-1/2" x 17-1/2" piece
  #3 - Cut (1) - 4-1/2" x 7-1/2" piece
  #2 - Cut (1) - 4-1/2" x 17-1/2" piece

- From 1/8 yd. of Green:
  #7 & #8 - Cut (2) - 1" x 7-1/2" pieces
  #5 & #6 - Cut (2) - 1" x 10-1/2" pieces

- From 1/4 yd. of Yellow (Binding):
  #10 - Cut (2) - 2-1/2" x 45" strips

- From 1/4 yd. of White:
  #9 - Cut (1) - 6-1/2" x 10-1/2" piece

Color a 6-1/2" x 10-1/2" Daisy Block as you did on the napkin. Piece together using 1/4" seams.

1. *Layer your quilt sandwich:*
   • Top - colored, pieced block
   • Middle - Batting
   • Bottom - Backing Fabric

2. *Baste* the layers together using either safety pins, basting pins or Sulky KK-2000 Temporary Spray Adhesive.

3. *Quilt*. Follow the previously listed steps for Thread Sketching, and use Sulky 30 wt. Blendables or solid color cotton threads to add your favorite quilting pattern to the border areas.

4. *Add Binding. (For detailed quilting and binding instructions, refer to the book, **Quick and Easy Weekend Quilting with Sulky** #900-B16.)*

Check out the Sulky Embroidery Club @ www.sulkyembclub.com for digitized, "Thread Sketch" Designs suitable for inking, like those below.

Daisy Chain

Needlecase

Hand Embroidered Bullion Roses
on Wool Felt with Sulky 12 wt. Blendables

by Maxine Ramey

Maxine has owned a quilt shop in Franklin, NC since 2005. This is the second fabric shop she has owned; the first was an heirloom sewing shop. She has sewn all her life, turning to quilting when her children became teens and no longer wanted hand-made garments. Styles and fabrics have changed so that home-sewn garments are desirable once again, so she is enjoying all types of sewing.

"Today's sewing requires many different applications and Sulky has a product to fit every situation. I love beautiful thread as much as I love beautiful fabric. Sulky Blendables are perfect for so many different things but I especially like them for handwork. The dependable variegation and the quality of the fibers always results in a successful project. I am confident that when I recommend a Sulky product to a customer they will be satisfied!" --- Maxine

Materials:

- Sewing Machine
- 1/4 yd. National Non-Woven™ Wool Felt for Booklet Cover
- 1/4 yd. Coordinating Wool Felt for Inside Pages
- Steam-a-Seam2™
- Sulky Fuse 'n Stitch™ and Heat-Away™ Clear Film Stabilizers
- Sulky KK 2000™ Temporary Spray Adhesive
- Sulky 12 wt. Blendables® Thread:
  Roses: #4047 Princess Garden
  Basket: #4046 Sweet Rose
  Leaves and Stems: #4101 Easter Eggs
- Sulky Polyester 60 wt. Black Bobbin Thread
- Milliner or Straw Needles, size 8
- 2 - 10" pieces of 1/4" Ribbon
- 2 Buttons
- Clover® Fine, White Marking Pen
- Fray Check™
- Pattern can be found on the CD in the back of this book

Create the Needlecase:

1. Cut 2 - 5" x 9" pieces of *Sulky Fuse 'n Stitch* and 2 - 5-1/2" x 9-1/2" pieces of wool felt.

2. Center a *Fuse 'n Stitch* piece on the wrong side of a felt piece and fuse them together. Repeat for the other pieces and set them aside for the lining.

3. Cut a 4" square of *Sulky Heat-Away Clear Film* Stabilizer and use a Clover fine, white marking pen to trace the basket, handles and vine stems onto it. Let dry.

4. Fold the wool felt in half like a booklet. Place the traced *Heat-Away* on the right side of the front, and center the design as you like it. (Remember that the felt will be trimmed later to make a 4" square Needle Case Booklet.) Temporarily adhere it in place with Sulky KK 2000.

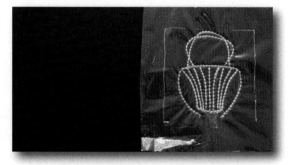

5. Thread the top of the sewing machine with Sulky 12 wt. Blendables Thread #4046 Sweet Rose. Put Sulky 60 wt. Polyester Bobbin Thread in the bobbin. Unfold the felt. Select a double straight stitch and sew on all of the traced basket and handle lines. Thread the top with 12 wt. Blendables #4101 Easter Eggs and stitch the vine and stems.

Hand Stitch the Roses:

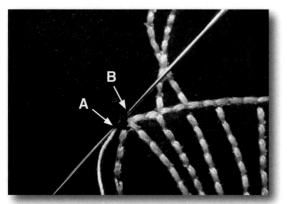

1. Remove the Heat-Away following package instructions. Work the Bullion Roses in Sulky 12 wt. #4047 Princess Garden. (See illustration of Back Stitch, Bullion Stitch, and Lazy Daisy Stitch on page 71.) Thread the straw needle with about 18" of thread. To secure the thread, make a backstitch on the back side in the center of the rose. Lay two bullion knots side by side, and then begin wrapping bullion knots around the two knots in a spiral until the series of knots looks like a rose.

To make a bullion stitch: bring the thread up at point A, place the needle in at point B, and bring the needle tip out again at point A. Leave the needle in the fabric as shown above.

2. Wrap the thread clockwise around the needle about 9 times with your working hand. Hold the wraps firmly with the

thumb and forefinger of your opposite hand. While still holding the wraps, pull the needle through and tug the needle upward fairly tightly. Let go of the wraps, and then tug the thread down close to the fabric in the direction you want the bullion to lay. Stitch through to the back side. Bring the needle up at the next point A and repeat the process. Work around the two center bullions in a spiral, tucking the point B end in close to the rose. When you are happy with the way the rose looks, take the thread to the back side and tie off. Remember, this is your rose and no two look alike!

Hand Stitch the Leaves:

1. Randomly work the leaves up and down the vines and around the roses with a lazy daisy stitch, which is worked by bringing the needle up from the back side at the base of the leaf. Then, send the needle to

the back again, allowing a very loose loop to form on top. Bring the needle up from the back at the tip of the leaf, stitching through the loop. Take the needle to the back again, catching the loop at the tip of the leaf.

2. No need to tie off after every leaf; you may work around the design, stitching as many leaves as your thread length allows. If you need to press your work, do so on the wrong side with the bullion embroidery placed face side down on a terry towel.

3. To finish the cover, spray KK 2000 onto the **Fuse 'n Stitch** side (underside) and adhere the underside of the other fused felt (lining) to it. Center the embroidery on the right half of the cover and trim the cover to 4" x 8" by using a ruler that is at least 4" x 8" and placing the 2" line (from the right side) on the center, stitched line of the basket. If your ruler is larger, simply trim two sides, turn the work and trim the remaining two.

Blanket Stitch the Cover:

1. Edge finish the outer edge of the Booklet Cover with either a blanket stitch by hand or a zig-zag satin stitch by machine (using a matching 30 wt. Blendables Thread in the bobbin).

Finish the Booklet:

1. Cut three pieces of coordinating wool felt for the inner pages. Cut one 4" x 8", one 3" x 7" and one 3" x 6-7/8". These sizes will allow the page edges to align evenly when closed.

2. Fuse the Steam-A-Seam2 onto the underside of the 4" x 8" wool felt and trim it to 3" x 7-1/8". Before removing the paper, fold in half with the paper side out and press to find the center.

3. Press the cover in half and press the pages in half to mark the centers. Align the pages inside and pin in place. Stitch down the center through all thicknesses to hold the pages inside the book.

Back Stitch

Bullion Stitch

Lazy Daisy Stitch

4. Attach ribbons to the front edge for ties. Tie them in a bow and trim to desired length. A dot of Fray Check on the cut ends will prevent unraveling.

Visit Maxine:
www.astitchintimenc.com

Her shop was featured in the January, 2011, issue of "Quilt Sampler Magazine".

Twisted Necklaces

by Sue Hausmann

"It has been a joy to work (or should I say play) with my friends at Sulky for over 20 years on the 'America Sews with Sue Hausmann' Public Television Series. Many people ask me how I am able to make all the projects we demonstrate on the shows and the answer is. 'I don't'. The guests make the projects they present and they prepare the demonstration steps. Some guests are kind enough to bring something for me to wear on the show that goes with the project! At the top of this list is Joyce Drexler! Joyce has been a guest on every America Sews series since it began in 1991. She not only brings me a jacket or shirt to wear, she leaves it with me to share with viewers in my trunk shows! One of the items Joyce brought many years ago was not the project for the day but an accessory to go with it. A necklace made from Sulky 12 weight Cotton Blendables Thread which was created with a twisting technique. This necklace was inspired by one Joyce saw that was made by Yvonne Perez-Collins. I was very excited because, for years, we had been teaching the twisted cord technique using the bobbin winder on the sewing machine to create ties, belts, cords, purse handles and 'sew' much more. I don't remember what the actual project was that we did on the show, but I have enjoyed the necklace that went with it. I've continued to wear it with many different colors and garments. The Sulky 12 weight Cotton Blendables Threads are fabulous for these projects because they have a beautiful sheen and they come in an incredible array of amazing color blends, each one more beautiful than the next! Joyce has personally designed the color combinations using her extensive art background to create these beautiful threads.!" . . . Sue

Inspired by a Twisted Thread Necklace made by Yvonne Perez-Collins and featured in the book,

"Sulky Secrets to Successful Embroidery" #900-B15. www.sulky.com

Materials:

- Sewing Machine with Bobbin Winding Spindle (or use a hand-held egg beater or Spinster™)

- 1 spool of Sulky 12 wt. Cotton Blendables Thread in the color of your choice (can make up to a 30" long, twisted-cord necklace)

- Optional: Small Beads to add or twist into the necklace

- Optional: Jewelry findings and tools for closure

Spinster

Measure:

1. Measure a favorite necklace to determine how long you would like yours to be. Sue likes the 28" to 30" length for a standard necklace and about an 18" length for a choker. There are no rules. You can make your necklace any length you desire.

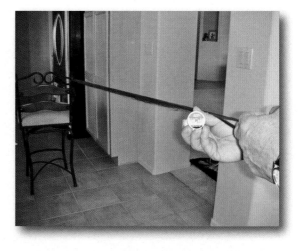

Create the Length desired:

"This is much easier if you can find a friend to help! Why not make two, one for each of you! Or, you can look for furniture, lamps or other items to wrap the lengths of thread around. We have stools with wrought iron decorative loops that worked perfectly when I wanted to create the lengths of thread wrap by myself." --- Sue

1. Hold the end of the thread and pull off 72" (Sue uses a yardstick to measure the first lengths) of Sulky 12 wt. Cotton Blendables Thread.

2. Hold the start end and have your friend take the other end. (Or wrap it around something.)

3. **DO NOT CUT THE THREAD.** Instead, pull the thread around her hand and walk away from her with the spool.

   Continue to pull the thread until the second length is 72", then wrap it around your hand. Continue to pull the thread off the spool, holding it to the 72" length, and hand it to your friend who will wrap it around her hand at the next 72" length.

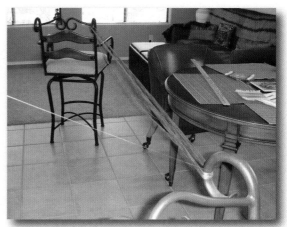

4. Continue to wrap these 72" lengths of thread (do not cut the thread) until you have about 150 lengths, or you use all the thread on the spool. Wow!

5. Keep the wraps taut unless you want a "loopy" effect in the finished, twisted cord, as on the multi-color necklace with beads. For the excess loops along the twisted cord, wrap loosely and let the thread "sag" in the wrapping step.

Twist the Thread Lengths:

1. Now the fun begins! You will need about a 12" length of the Sulky 12 wt. Cotton Blendables Thread (any color) doubled.

2. Wrap it around one end of the thread wraps, close to the end, and tie a square knot in it that will not pull out. This will give you a "handle" on one end of your 72" wrapped lengths.

3. Put the short thread end through the hole in a sewing machine bobbin from the outside in, and put the bobbin on the bobbin winder spindle on your sewing machine so the wrapped lengths are on the outside.

4. This is where you need a second person to hold the end of the threads out away from the sewing machine while you turn on the

bobbin winder.

5. For more control, set the bobbin winding for slow to medium speed. As the bobbin winder turns, it turns the end of the threads, twisting them. When the person at the other end feels a tug on the threads, stop the bobbin winding. The thread strands should be twisted smooth and tight.

Sue's bobbin winder is on top of her machine with a button on the screen to start winding. If your bobbin winder is in another location and you need to step on the foot control to wind, that is fine too. Run the machine as you would when winding a bobbin, however, there is no thread being wound on the bobbin. The thread wrap lengths will be twisted outside the bobbin instead.

Other ways to Twist:

Another way to twist the thread is to use your electric or manual egg beater from the kitchen. Tie one end of the thread wrap to the beater and run the beater at a slow speed to twist the threads.

Or, use the Spinster.

Double the Twisted Threads:

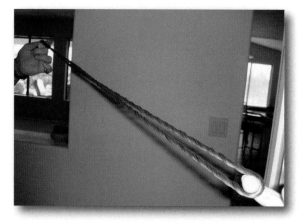

1. To create the double twisted thread, take the end of the twisted thread off the bobbin winder or egg beater. Hold the twisted threads as straight as possible and pinch and hold the center of the thread length.

2. Hand the end you are holding to the person holding the other end and pull the center toward you.

3. Once it is fairly straight, LET GO OF THE CENTER END. The twisted threads will "squiggle-up", twisting back on themselves. Smooth the threads out and, WOW, you have a beautiful Sulky Blendables Twisted Cord!

Options:

"I love the beauty and simplicity of having just the thread in my Sulky Blendables Twisted Cord Necklaces, however, you may want to add details to the necklace with a string of beads or a chain, etc." --- Sue

1. String beads onto two strands of Sulky 30 wt. Cotton Thread and lay them into the thread wrap before twisting. It is even easier to wrap the beads around the finished necklace and catch it in the closure at the end. Since one-sided rhinestones do not lay *"right side out"* unless you really work at it, just use beads.

Finish the ends of your necklace with a closure. The simplicity of creating a large knot "button" on one end to slip through the "loop" created by the twisted threads on the other end works beautifully. Of course, you can also use jewelry closures on your necklace. ---- *Enjoy!*

Braided Uni-Sex Friendship Bracelets

by Amber Drexler

"My grandma, Joyce Drexler, introduced me to Sulky Blendables Threads years ago when she first designed them. I loved the way the colors flowed into one another and the fact that there were so many from which to choose. It gave me an idea for making Friendship Bracelets, Necklaces and Ankle Bracelets. I started playing around with the threads and found it was really cool to combine hanks of the thread and then braid them.

I would sit in front of the TV and make them for my friends! It was so much fun that it became addictive! I made them for everyone I knew!

Amber and her boyfriend Stephen. Amber is wearing a glass heart (that Stephen gave her) on one of her braided cords and Stephen is wearing a bracelet (that Amber made for him) that wraps around twice.

Then I helped my grandpa at a Trade Show in Orlando where I started explaining how to make them to customers. A few people asked if I would make some for them to buy, and I did!

It's a quick and easy way to let friends know you care about them. I made several for my boyfriend and he wears all of them, all together, all the time. He just knotted the ends so they would not come off. The bracelets let the other girls know that he's taken and loved! If you have someone you know who is going through breast cancer treatment, make them a pink bracelet to wear, so they always know you care and are praying for them to recover." --- Amber

Make longer lengths and wrap them twice around your wrists or ankles.

Go wild and make them to braid into your hair.

They are perfect for:
* zipper pulls
* key chains
* shoelaces
* headbands too!

They are fun to make and fun to wear.

Measure:

1. Loosely measure your friend's wrist with a tape measure, or measure a bracelet that they wear.

2. Add four inches and cut the number of lengths of heavyweight Sulky 12 wt. Solid Color Cotton or Blendables that you desire. If you plan on double or triple wrapping it, then increase the amount as needed.

Braid:

1. You determine how thick the bracelet will be by how many lengths of thread you use in each bundle of three that are needed for braiding. Amber used 30 strands in each of the three color groups for the bracelet above. You can also add strings of beads, stones, shells, charms, etc., to any of the three bundles of thread, if desired.

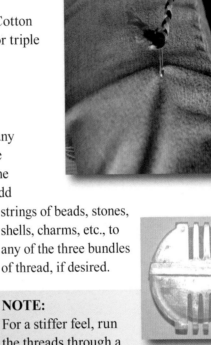

NOTE:
For a stiffer feel, run the threads through a beeswax holder before knotting them together. This works well when stringing beads etc., on the thread.

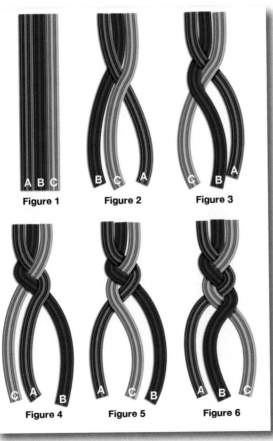

Figure 1   Figure 2   Figure 3

Figure 4   Figure 5   Figure 6

2. Knot the 3 bundles together at one end, then use a safety pin to pin that end to your jeans, etc.; begin to braid by following the illustrations on the left.

3. When you are done braiding, tie the three ends together. Then, wrap the braided cord around your friend's wrist, ankle, etc., and tie the ends in a knot, or use jewelry closures to finish.

Friendship Bracelets

Charity Bracelets

by Terri Stenger

"My interest in friendship bracelets was born when my daughter Lauren began middle school and her cousin showed us how to make them using embroidery floss. When our friend Sandy saw Lauren's bracelets and realized I made them, she asked if I would be interested in selling them in her coffee shop. We hit on the idea of offering the bracelets as a means to raise funds for scholarships for our summer swim team, the Franklin Amateur Swim Team (FAST) which my husband and I had been involved with when Lauren was younger. This year we are using the proceeds to put at least 6 kids on the team who otherwise wouldn't be able to afford the fees to join.

When Joyce asked if I would make some bracelets using Sulky 12 wt. Cotton Threads in Solid Colors and Blendables for this book, I agreed in exchange for a contribution to FAST. It was so much easier using the Sulky thread on spools instead of floss, and they turned out very nice. I increased the amount of strands used. The Blendables multi-color combinations made the bracelets really unique." --- Terri

"I use the Klutz Book, Friendship Bracelets by Laura Torres. Published by Klutz, ©2011 Klutz, Palo Alto, CA 94306. Used by permission of Klutz." --- Terri

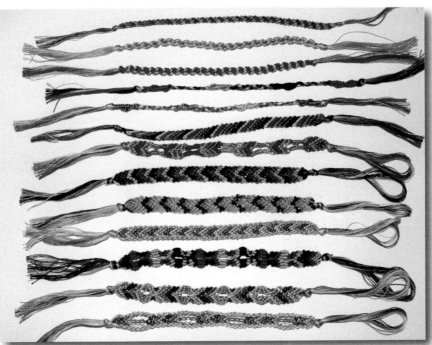

What a great way to raise funds for your favorite charity!

Punch Needle Mitten Coasters

by Connie Kauffman - Designer / Author

"I found it a real joy to do Punch Needle using Sulky Cotton Threads. No separating strands of thread like when using embroidery floss! I also found I was able to use LONG lengths of thread (2 to 3 yards, doubled to about 1-1/2 yard lengths) because the thread is so smooth and tangle-free. This made for fewer needle threadings! I love the soft, mottled look that the Sulky Blendables give to punch needle designs." --- Connie

Connie Kauffman is a quilt designer, author and teacher who lives in Nappanee, IN. She has authored 5 quilting books and has had many designs published in other books and magazines. She has her own pattern line called Kauffman Designs.

Check out her website at www.conniekauffman.com.

Materials:

- Mitten Pattern and Color Guide found on the CD in the back of this book
- 2 - 7" squares of Weaver's Cloth
- Punch Needle
- Small Embroidery Hoop (5" diameter)
- Sulky Iron-On Transfer Pens: Red, Yellow, Green, Brown, and Black
- Sulky 12 wt. Cotton Blendables:
  #4057 Fresh Butter, #4044 Butterscotch, #4050 Pine Palette, #4042 Redwork and #4053 Falling Leaves
- Sulky 30 wt. Cotton Thread #1005 Black
- Sulky 12 wt. Cotton Thread #1001 White
- Any inexpensive paper such as copy paper or loose-leaf paper
- 6" x 8" non-adhesive, rubber-backed Shelf Liner

Transfer the Mitten Design:

1. To make a color-coded pattern, use the 5 different colors of Sulky Iron-on Transfer Pens listed above to trace the mitten pattern (found on the CD in the back of this book) onto any inexpensive paper, like copy paper. If you want a matched "pair" of mittens, then use a window or a light box to trace one in reverse.

2. Following the instructions on the Sulky Iron-On Transfer Pen package, iron the transfer onto the weaver's cloth (two, if you are making a pair).

Punch the Mitten Design:

1. Use a double strand of Sulky 12 wt. Blendables thread for all colors, except use one strand of Sulky 30 wt. Solid for the black lines. Follow the instructions for using the punch needle, and follow the color guide for the thread colors.

2. Start in the center of the star and work your way around the star and mitten.

3. When making the cuff, punch the rows going up and down, then add the black lines last.

Construct the Mitten Coaster:

1. When complete, remove from the hoop and trim the fabric, leaving a 1/4" seam allowance all around the edge of the mitten. Clip carefully into the thumb and cuff area. *(If this seems to fray a lot, add a dot of Fray Check or white glue.)*

2. Fold the cloth edges under and hand whip-stitch them to the back of the mitten so that the edges are not visible from the front.

3. Trace the outside edge of the pattern onto the rubber-backed shelf liner and cut out just outside the drawn lines. Place the liner pieces on the back of the mittens. Using small stitches, whip-stitch the liner to the back of the mitten.

HINT: *If the edge of the fabric or the edge of the shelf liner peeks out from under the mitten coaster, use a permanent, red, Sharpie marker to cover the edges.*

Tissue Box

by Nancy Sapin and Joyce Drexler

"The moss on the roof, made by serging off Blendables #4020 Moss Medley, added a great touch, and the embellished panels of fabric gave it the earthy quality we were looking for." --- Joyce

Materials:

- Zig-zag Sewing Machine
- Machine Needles: 16/100 Jeans Needle and 14/90 Topstitch Needle
- Closed-toe Appliqué Foot
- Free-Motion, Spring-type, Open-toe Foot
- Jeans-A-Ma-Jig™ accessory
- Wooden Skewer
- Straight Pins
- Sharp-Pointed Scissors
- Quilter's 12" Ruler
- 60 mm Rotary Cutter and Mat
- Acid-free Glue Stick
- Steam-A-Seam2™ or Lite
- Steam Iron and Pad
- Sharpie Fine-Line, Permanent-Ink Marker
- 8" roll of Sulky Fuse 'n Stitch™
- 1 yard packages of Sulky Soft 'n Sheer Extra™ and Sulky Tear-Easy™ Stabilizers
- Sulky 30 wt. Cotton Blendables® Thread that complements your chosen fabric
- Sulky 60 wt. White Polyester Bobbin Thread - for the Base only
- Sulky KK 2000™ Temporary Spray Adhesive
- 1/2 yd. fabric (for fronts, sides & ground)
- 1/4 yd. fabric (for roof & trim)
- 1 - 100 foot package of cotton clothesline
- 1 - 50 foot package of cotton clothesline
- 5" x 8-1/2" piece of card stock

Set up your Machine:

- Attach a closed-toe appliqué foot
- Insert a 14/90 topstitch needle
- Thread the top and bobbin with Sulky White Bobbin Thread
- Select a zig-zag stitch
- Adjust the width - medium to small
- Select a medium length

Basic Construction:

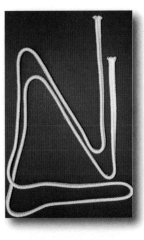

1. Fold 100 feet of clothesline in half.

   Starting at the cut ends, hold both pieces side-by-side, close together, and zig-zag them together.

2. Cut this joined piece in half when you near the fold in your clothesline.

   Fold in half again and, starting at the cut ends, zig-zag these sections together.

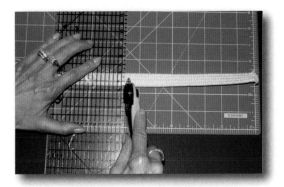

3. Cut in half when you approach the fold. You now have 4 pieces that are zig-zagged together.

Front and Back Panels:

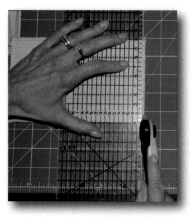

to 7-1/2" long *(always even out both ends to reach your desired measurement).* Repeat to construct the back panel the same as the front panel.

1. Cut five 7-3/4" long pieces from the 4-across, zig-zagged strip. Cut two single 7-3/4" pieces from a new package of clothesline, and zig-zag them together.

2. Zig-zag all of them together, making 22 cords across.

It should measure 4-1/2" across.

This will construct the **Front Panel.** *(You can always add or substract a cord to meet your desired width measurement.)*

3. Use a 60 mm Rotary Cutter and Quilter's Ruler to trim the panels

4. Cut 4 pieces of **Sulky Fuse 'n-Stitch** Stabilizer just slightly shy of 4-1/2" x 7-1/2" *(so it sits just inside the front and back panels).*

5. Use a medium cotton setting and a dry iron to fuse one

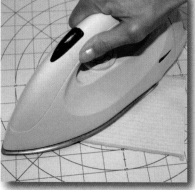

piece of **Fuse 'n Stitch** *(the shiny side is the fusible side)* to each side of both panels. Press and hold the iron down until each piece is completely fused.

6. Trace the roof pitch template (found on the CD) onto card stock paper and cut it out.

Place your template on the two stabilized panels and use the Sharpie marker to draw your pitch lines so that the top pitch is in the center.

7. Use a 60 mm Rotary Cutter and Quilter's Ruler to cut the roof pitches so both front and back panels are the same.

Side Panels:

1. Cut five 5-1/4" long pieces from the 4-across, zig-zagged strip. Zig-zag all 5 together.

2. Cut one 5-1/4" piece from the second package of clothesline and zig-zag it onto the 20-across piece, making it 21 cords across.

It should measure 4-1/4" across. This will construct the **Side Panel.** *(You can always add or substract a cord to meet your desired width measurement.)*

3. Repeat to construct the opposite **Side Panel.**

4. Use a 60 mm Rotary Cutter and Quilter's Ruler to trim the panels to 5" long *(always even out both pieces to reach your desired measurement).*

5. Cut 4 pieces of ***Sulky Fuse-'n Stitch Stabilizer*** just slightly shy of 4-1/4" x 5" each (so it sits inside your **Side Panels).**

6. Use a medium cotton setting and a dry iron to fuse one piece of ***Fuse-'n Stitch*** (the shiny side is the fusible side) to each side of both panels.

Press and hold the iron down until each piece is completely fused.

Roof Panels:

1. Cut six, 7-1/4" long pieces from the 4-across, zig-zagged strip. Zig-zag all 6 together. It should measure about 5" across. This will construct one **Roof Panel.** Repeat to construct the opposite **Roof Panel.**

2. Use a 60 mm Rotary Cutter and Quilter's Ruler to trim the panels to 7" long *(always even out both ends to reach your desired measurement).*

3. Cut 4 pieces of ***Sulky Fuse-'n Stitch Stabilizer*** just slightly shy of 5" x 7" each (so it sits inside the roof panels).

Follow fusing directions in Step 6 of Side Panel directions.

Bottom Base Panel:

1. Cut nine, 7-3/4" long pieces from the 4-across, zig-zagged strip. Zig-zag all 9 together. It should measure about 7-1/2" across.

2. Use a 60 mm Rotary Cutter and Quilter's Ruler to trim the base to about 7-1/2" square *(always even out both ends to reach your desired measurement)*.

3. Cut 2 pieces of **Sulky Fuse 'n Stitch Stabilizer** just slightly shy of 7-1/2" square (so it sits inside the bottom base). *Follow previous fusing directions.*

Choosing the Fabric for your Birdhouse:

Look for fabrics for the front, back and sides that can make an exciting birdhouse. Fabrics that look painted work best and are easiest to thread paint. Border fabrics can also be used if the motifs are proportional to the size of the birdhouse.

Use a coordinating fabric for the appliquéd bird hole. Look at the darkest background color in the chosen front panel fabric and try to match it.

Choose a color in the painted panels that can become the roof, maybe an interesting batik that picks up some of the darkest background colors, or the same fabric as your bird hole and trim.

If you can't make up your mind, choose one fabric for the inside and another for the outside. The roof can then become reversible.

Choose the bottom base fabric by seeing what colors are at the base of the thread painted house fabric. This panel can also become reversible.

Set up your Machine for Thread Painting:

- Attach an open-toe, spring-action, free-motion foot

- Insert a 14/90 topstitch, embroidery, or metallic needle

- Thread the top and bobbin with Sulky 30 wt. Blendables Thread

- Drop or cover the feed dogs (teeth)

- Select a free-motion straight stitch

HINT:

*It's best **NOT** to cut the fabric at this time because it's easier to thread paint larger pieces. Place the base panels under the stabilized fabric, arrange the base exactly where you want it and place some pieces of masking tape around the edges so you will know to only thread color within the boundaries.*

1. Choose the fabric area that you want to display on the front and back panels. Fuse a 7" x 9" piece of **Sulky Soft 'n Sheer Extra** (the rough side is the fusible side) onto the wrong side of the fabric display areas. Spray Sulky KK 2000 onto a 7" x 9" piece of **Sulky Tear-Easy** and place it over the **Soft 'n Sheer Extra.**

colors of Sulky 30 wt. Blendables to accent the colors in the fabric.

Thread Painting uses the needle like a crayon with the thread being the color. Find your rhythm so the stitches become balanced and even. When you scribble or make circles, straight lines, and outline stitching, it will take you right back to childhood.

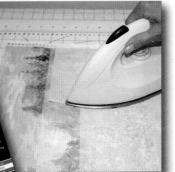

2. Flip the fabric over and place it under the needle. Take one stitch and bring the bobbin thread up to the top. Begin straight stitch thread painting from the background to the foreground, using different

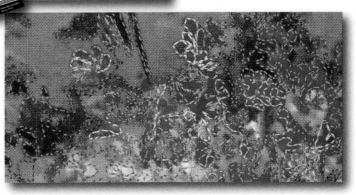

Appliqué the Birdhouse Hole:

1. Use a Sharpie, fine-line, permanent-ink marker to draw a circle on the rough (fusible) side of **Sulky Soft 'n Sheer Extra** by tracing around the end of a Sulky Blendables spool of thread.

2. Place the traced circle, rough side up, on the right side of the chosen accent fabric.

3. Slowly free-motion straight stitch around the circle by following the drawn line, or straight stitch one stitch, turn, stitch, turn, stitch, etc. Use sharp-pointed scissors to cut out the stitched circle about 1/8" beyond the stitch lines.

4. Make a cut in the **Soft 'n Sheer Extra** and turn the stabilizer under, using a point turner or bodkin to smooth out the edges. The fusible side of the **Soft 'n Sheer Extra** is now turned under and against the wrong side of the circle. Make sure your circle is still smooth and round. Slowly fuse so you now have a turned, round appliqué.

Lightly spray Sulky KK 2000 onto the stabilizer side of the circle and place it according to the pitch template.

(Place the template over the thread painted fabric display area. Stick a straight

pin in the center of the bird hole, lift the template and mark the fabric for proper placement.)

Set up the Machine for Blanket Stitching:

- Attach a closed-toe appliqué foot
- Insert a 14/90 topstitch needle
- Thread the top and bobbin with Sulky Blendables to match the fabric
- Select a blanket stitch
- Choose your preferred width and length

1. Slowly blanket stitch the appliquéd bird hole while turning the fabric slightly every stitch or two.

2. When you are finished, carefully tear away the **Tear-Easy Stabilizer**.

Apply Sulky Soft 'n Sheer Extra to the Birdhouse Panels:

1. For a more finished look, we will fuse **Sulky Soft 'n Sheer Extra** onto the inside of the 2 sides of each panel and the front and back panels.

2. Cut two 5-1/2" x 8-1/2" and two 5" x 6" pieces of **Sulky Soft 'n Sheer Extra.**

Center and fuse the **Soft 'n Sheer Extra** (the bumpy side is the fusible side) onto the inside of each of the 4 panels.

HINT: *Place a piece of painter's tape on the Soft 'n Sheer Extra so you do not confuse the inside and front of each panel.*

3. Use a medium hot iron to roll the side of the **Soft 'n Sheer Extra** to the side of each of the panels, then finger press to set. Trim even to the front. Pinch and clip all corners.

Apply the Embellished Fabric to the Base Panels:

1. Cut two 5-1/2" x 8-1/2" pieces of Steam-a-Seam2. Fuse one to the wrong side of each of your thread-colored front and back panel fabrics.

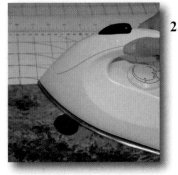

2. Center or "fussyplace" the front clothesline panel (**Soft-'n Sheer Extra** side up so you

see the painter's tape) in the center of the Steam-a-Seam2, with the birdhouse hole centered on the front fabric according to the template. Use steam to fuse the front panel fabric to the top of the base panel.

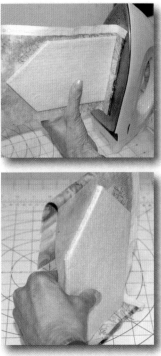

3. Use a medium hot iron to roll and fuse the side of the fabric to the side of the panel; cool slightly and trim even to the panel.

4. Repeat for all sides and roof pitch so the fabric flows from the front to the back.

5. Pinch and clip all corner tabs as you go. Repeat this on the back panel with the second piece of prepared fabric.

6. Cut two 5" x 6" pieces of Steam-a-Seam2 for both side panels. Repeat as before, fusing the fronts and all sides. Set these panels aside for now.

Roof Fabric:

Fusible on wrong side

Release Sheet

1. Cut four 6" x 8" pieces from one fabric or, for a reversible roof, cut 2 pieces each from two different fabrics.

2. Cut four 6" x 8" pieces of Steam-a-Seam2 and fuse them onto the wrong side of your fabric choices. First, fuse on what will be the inside of your roof panels (in the same manner as you fused the birdhouse panels on the previous page), along with fusing the sides. Trim.

Right side of fabric rolled over the edge

3. Fuse the front fabric to the opposite side of the roof panel. As each side edge is fused, it will fuse over the inside fabric side edge so the fabric flows from the front to the back. Trim. This will give the front side a more finished look. Repeat this for the second roof panel.

Apply the Roof Trim and make the Tissue Opening:

Set up the Machine:

• Attach a closed-toe appliqué foot

• Insert a 16/100 denim or topstitch needle

• Thread the top and bobbin with a Sulky 30 wt. Cotton Blendables Thread that coordinates with your fabric

• Select a multi-stitch zig-zag with a medium width and length

1. Choose the fabric for the trim strips (Nancy chose a solid brown like the inside of the roof).

2. To trim the roof, it will take about 58" of clothesline wrapped with 1" strips of fabric.

Clothesline Wrapping Instructions:

To Begin Wrapping:

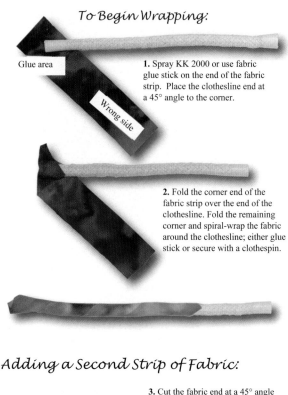

Glue area

Wrong side

1. Spray KK 2000 or use fabric glue stick on the end of the fabric strip. Place the clothesline end at a 45° angle to the corner.

2. Fold the corner end of the fabric strip over the end of the clothesline. Fold the remaining corner and spiral-wrap the fabric around the clothesline; either glue stick or secure with a clothespin.

Adding a Second Strip of Fabric:

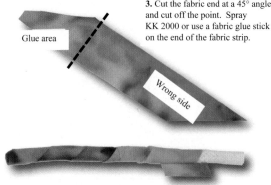

Glue area

Wrong side

3. Cut the fabric end at a 45° angle and cut off the point. Spray KK 2000 or use a fabric glue stick on the end of the fabric strip.

When both ends need to be finished:

1. Spray KK 2000 or use a fabric glue stick on the end of the fabric strip. Place the clothesline end at a 45° angle to the corner.

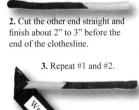

2. Cut the other end straight and finish about 2" to 3" before the end of the clothesline.

4. Cut and glue the fabric end so it overlaps one wrap beyond the last.

3. Repeat #1 and #2.

Glue area

Wrong side

5. Both ends now have a finished look. This is how you make the 2 "spacers" below.

3. Cut and wrap two 2" lengths of clothesline, which will be used later as *"spacers"* to form the opening for the tissue to come through the roof.

4. Begin by pinning, then zig-zagging the first section of the 58" wrapped cord to the inside corner, which becomes the top of the roof. Support the back of the foot with a Jeans-A-Ma-Jig accessory so you can stitch on the edge.

5. At the corners, leave the needle down in the center of the wrapped cord and pivot, lining up the next edge of the panel. Repeat this process for all of the edges.

6. As you approach where you began, add one piece of the 2" wrapped *"spacer"* cord, butting it up lengthwise against the sewn cord. Place another wrapped *"spacer"* next to the 2" piece of wrapped cord (this will be where the end of the long wrapped clothesline will

Spacer

finish). Zig-zag past the 2" wrapped cord, catching the cord, but not the *"spacer"*.

7. Continue to stitch on the wrapped cord along the 5" side of the second roof panel, pivot at the corner and stitch the 7" side, pivot and stitch along the last 5" side, then pivot and STOP.

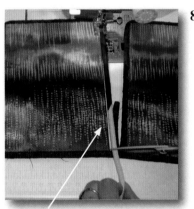

Stop wrapping here. Cut clothesline as shown. Wrap remaining piece of clothesline from the bottom up.

8. Follow the previous instructions for ending the clothesline wrap; stopping the wrap in the center, gluing, cutting the cord at the end of the 7" side, and finishing the clothesline end by starting with a new strip and finishing again by overlapping and gluing in the center.

9. Continue to zig-zag to the end of the 7" side that will be the top of the roof. Stop with the needle down and pivot. Zig-zag to attach the 2" strip, turn and zig-zag the second side of the 2" strip to attach both roof panels together.

10. Attach the second 2" *"spacer"* strip to the opposite end of the 7" roof top by zig-zagging it in place. Stitch in place a couple of stitches to finish. The center roof hole will become the tissue dispenser. The roof will now easily hinge over the birdhouse pitch once it is completed.

Add the Wrapped Trim to the Front Panel:

1. It will take about 44" of clothesline wrapped with 1" strips of coordinating fabric to trim out your panels.

Set up the Machine:
- Attach a closed-toe appliqué foot

- Insert a 16/100 denim needle

- Thread the top and bobbin with a Sulky 30 wt. Cotton Blendables that coordinates with your fabric choice

- Select a multi-stitch zig-zag with a medium width and length

1. Turn the roof pitch toward you with the front panel to the left of the needle. Place the end of the wrapped cord at the bottom of the front panel, leaving the end extending just slightly past the corner because it tends to pull back just a bit, and the very end is mostly fabric that will compress.

2. Use two straight pins to hold the wrapped clothesline snug against the side of the panel so it doesn't slip. Place a Jeans-a-Ma-Jig accessory under the back side to level the presser foot.

3. As you begin stitching, remove the straight pins and use a stiletto or bamboo skewer to hold the cord flat to the panel side as you continue to stitch.

4. When you arrive at the angle of the pitch, stop with the needle down in the center of the presser foot. Turn and replace the Jeans-a-Ma-Jig (if necessary) under the back side to level the presser foot. Continue stitching.

5. Repeat as you turn each corner.

6. Once you turn the last corner, just past the second pitch and headed down the other side, STOP with the needle in the down position.

7. Before you finish wrapping, cut the clothesline cord so it is even with the BOTTOM of the side. End the fabric wrap halfway down the side by cutting it square, using a glue stick to glue the fabric end, and securing it to the clothesline.

8. At the end of the cord, begin wrapping the fabric strip onto it like you started wrapping at the beginning. (You are now working backwards toward the glued fabric end.) As you approach the glued fabric end, cut your fabric strip so it will wrap one time past the glued end on the cord, again cutting the fabric strip square and gluing the end so it sticks to the fabric and no cord shows through. This gives you a finished beginning and end.

9. Continue stitching down the side to the bottom of the panel and the end of the cord. Stitch in place a couple of stitches to finish. Repeat this process on the back panel.

Add the Wrapped Trim to the Side Panels:

1. Cut two 4-1/4" pieces of clothesline.

2. Wrap the cord in the same manner as above so both ends are finished and the fabric overlaps in the center.

3. Zig-zag this strip onto each top of the side panels, beginning the same way as the front panel. Finish off.

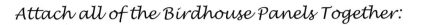

Attach all of the Birdhouse Panels Together:

1. Place the panels arranged in a straight line, back, side, front, side.

2. Working from the left to the right, line up both bottoms so they are even and zig-zag the side to the back panel. Then zig-zag the other side panel to the front panel.

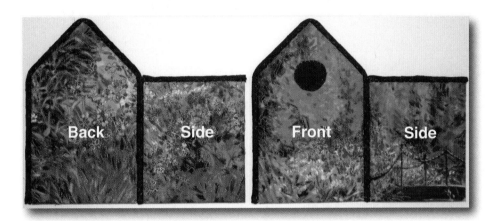

3. Zig-zag the back's side panel onto the front panel, lining up the bottoms so they are even.

4. Hinge all 4 panels to make a box. You will need to HAND STITCH the side and back panels together. Line up the bottoms and use an invisible zig-zag hand stitch, possibly using needle-nose pliers to assist in pulling the needle.

5. The birdhouse panels are now finished and trimmed, and the tissue box should slide in easily.

Build the Ground Base:

1. Cut nine 7-3/4" strips from your 4-strip clothesline and stitch them together. Trim both ends to 7-1/2" square. Cut two pieces of **Fuse 'n Stitch** just slightly shy of 7-1/2" square and fuse them onto each side of the clothesline base.

2. Cut two 8-1/2" squares of Steam-a-Seam2 and fuse them onto the back of the chosen 8-1/2" fabric squares. Following the previous fusing instructions, fuse the fabric to the back of the base first and then to the front.

3. To stitch 2 rows around the ground base, you will need approximately 67" of clothesline wrapped with 1" strips of fabric.

4. Begin on a corner and stitch down the first side (follow the same instructions as for the roof), turn (remember to keep your presser foot level with each turn), stitch, turn, stitch and turn again past the corner where you began.

5. Add one more row to make a total of two rows. When you turn the last corner and approach the corner where you started, STOP!

6. To finish, cut your clothesline at a long angle at the corner where you began. Wrap almost to the end and use glue stick on about the last 2 inches of the fabric. Wrap the fabric strip tightly around and past the end of the clothesline, angling it into a fabric taper. Zig-zag off the tapered end. Place the fabric birdhouse straight or on an angle to the bottom base.

Check out Nancy's Specialty Boxes ---
Instructions For a Toilet Paper Holder and "Whatever" Box can be found on the CD in the back of this book.

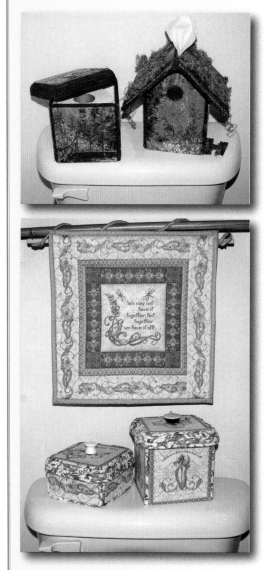

Nancy used printed panels that she thread painted.

Tissue Box

It's time to think about what type of embellishments you might wish to add; something that enhances your fabric choices. Now, you know that everyone who sees this will want one, so be prepared to make several. You can make one to match a quilt, add a beautiful embroidery to the front or roof panels, add beads, chimes and just go CRAZY. It's a birdhouse after all.

Here's what some of the National Sulky Educators did on their Birdhouse Tissue Boxes ---

Ellen Osten
"Happy Birdie To You"

"One of my favorite things is looking out of the window of my sewing studio and watching all the birds, butterflies and squirrels; along with birthday cake and cupcakes, these are a couple of things that always make me smile. When it came time to choose a birdhouse theme, I just happened to have my birthday fabric collection laying on the cutting table, so everything just came to be. Add a little bit of this and that, Sulky Holoshimmer and Blendables, the Fairy Birthday Princess and, of course, THOMAS, my son's tabby cat who always adds a little drama. The footed pedestal for *Happy Birdie To You* completes the set."
--- Ellen

Diane Gloystein
"As an afficionado of creating wearable art, I sometimes forget to let my hair down and take a break from the intensity of clothing construction and just enjoy crafting. This project was so much fun to make! I had forgotten how useful glue can be! When I saw this adorable birdhouse project, designed by Nancy Sapin, I knew immediately that I wanted to re-engineer those straight lines into a wonky birdhouse. And, of course, I can't imagine using anything other than my favorite fabric…Silk Dupioni! I love the whimsical beaded flowers growing in front of my house. The 12 wt. Sulky Cotton Blendables #4106 Primaries adds colorful magic to the doodles stitched on the house and shingles! And there's nothing like a touch of black and white to make those bright colors sizzle!" --- Diane

Pat Welch

"We usually think of birdhouses and springtime together. When I began my birdhouse in the winter, I looked out into the backyard and saw the wrens going in and out of their little house in the snow. So I decided to make mine a winter theme. I used Sulky Blendables to sew the house together, and Sulky Sliver #8040 Opalescent for the roof because it picks up and reflects other colors and looks just like real snow." --- Pat

Lee Fletcher

"I wanted to demonstrate how beautifully the Sulky 30 wt. Blendables work with digitized machine embroidery. I simply stitched out the designs on organza, trimmed the organza away, and fused them onto the birdhouse with a lightweight, double-sided fusible web. I loved the dimension that the heavier thread gave the embroidery." --- Lee

Suzy Seed

"I used Sulky 12 wt. Blendables in the needle and a Sulky metallic in the bobbin to create needle lace on Super Solvy for the roof. The small pieces of needle lace were done the same way for placement on other parts of the birdhouse. I did a mossing stitch and decorative stitching with a leaf pattern using Sulky 30 wt. Blendables. The fabric was hand-dyed and it was the perfect color for me to use as a backdrop for the threads." --- Suzy

Eric Drexler

"I was so inspired by Nancy's birdhouse design, I had to play along and make one like hers. I have been wanting to dabble in free-motion landscapes, and this was a perfect size to start with. Although I didn't go so far as to make all four seasons, the 30 wt. Blendables made this landscape come to life and easily blended with all the colors of the flowers, grasses, and scenery." --- Eric

Nancy's Four Seasons Birdhouse Tissue Boxes:

Nancy Sapin

"I had a wonderful time designing these birdhouse tissue boxes. Thank you Joyce for conceiving the idea." --- Nancy

Summer

"The first one I designed is what I call my Summer Birdhouse. For years I had these fabric panels that were waiting for just the right idea to come along, and this was it. *Sulky Soft-'n Sheer Extra* made it possible to thread paint the fabric (using many different Sulky 30 wt. Blendables) and keep the fabric pliable enough to wrap the sides of a clothesline base. After finishing, I had these serged, end pieces left over in a wad from a previous job that reminded me of moss. I serged a few more strips of Blendables #4020 Moss Medley and, VOILÀ, moss on the roof."

Spring

"The second birdhouse that I made was the lamb fabric border print, with some coordinates. It made a beautiful Spring thread painted birdhouse. I completed it with just an added touch of thread-grass, made from Blendables #4019 Forest Floor, attached to the corners. Now, I was on a mission to create all four seasons."

Autumn

"I was now on the hunt for just the right Autumn fabric, and I found it in Joyce's stash. I decided to do my thread work on the roof this time instead of thread painting the side panels. I thread painted the leaf fabric with 12 wt. Blendables #4010 Carmel Apple and made some 3-D leaves flapping in the breeze (two pieces of fabric between Steam-a-Seam2) for that real Autumn look. I usually love making leaves the way Heidi Lund did on page 39 in the book **An Updated Supplement to Sulky's Secrets to Successful Stabilizing** (#900-B17). However, now that *Sulky Sticky Fabri-Solvy* is on the market, I found clip-art leaves on the computer, arranged them on a page, and printed them on printable *Sticky Fabri-Solvy.* I peeled off the back and placed the stabilizer on sheer silk organza. Without hooping, I was able to quickly free-motion stitch the leaves, cut them all out, wash out the *Sticky Fabri-Solvy*, and let them dry as if they had just fallen from the tree. By just adding some of the wonderful embellishing techniques found within the pages of various Sulky books, knowing the beautiful outcome Sulky Blendables create, and realizing that with each new stabilizer that Sulky introduces, the rules change and our options broaden, making more projects easier."

Winter

"I practiced making faux fur from page 91 of the book, **Sew, Craft, Quilt & Embroider Confidently with Sulky Stabilizers** (#900-B19), and thought that technique could make beautiful snow. I also had these winter fabric panels just waiting for the right project. Because I was making snow panels an exact size, I chose to use *Sulky Fabri-Solvy* under and over my sheer base with various white yarns, cotton pieces, loose white rayon threads, and a bit of Angelina™ fibers all encased within. I stitched it all together using Sulky Sliver #8040 Opalescent and Sulky 30 wt. Rayon #1001 Bright White. After washing out the *Solvy* and allowing it to dry, it was just perfect for roof snow. Then, I accented the snow-scene fabric with my chosen Blendables by thread painting on the birdhouse sides. Thus, there was snow on the roof of my winter birdhouse design, with some extra placed here and there. Then, I just had to make a cottonball snowman to complete the look." ---Nancy

Tissue Box

Shoulder Bag

by Nancy Sapin
National Sulky Educator & Designer

Finished Size: 7" x 14" plus handles.

Materials:

- Zig-zag Sewing Machine
- 16/100 Jeans Needle
- Closed-toe Appliqué Foot
- Zipper Foot - *for sewing handles in place*
- Jeans-A-Ma-Jig™ Accessory
- Wooden Skewer
- Straight Pins
- Sharp, pointed Scissors
- 12" Quilter's Ruler
- 60 mm Rotary Cutter and Mat
- Masking Tape
- Acid-free Glue Stick

- Steam-A-Seam2™ or Lite Steam-A-Seam2
- Steam Iron and Pad
- 1 yard from an 8" roll of Sulky Fuse 'n Stitch™
- Sulky 30 wt. Cotton Blendables® Thread that complements your chosen fabric
- Sulky KK 2000™ Temporary Spray Adhesive
- 1/4 yd. fabric (for base & top 3 rows)
- 1 yd. fabric (for purse body & handles)
- 1 - 100 foot package of cotton clothesline
- *(This purse used about 18 - 1" strips of fabric, depending on how tightly you wrap.)*
- 1 - Large Decorative Button
- Sulky White Polyester Bobbin Thread

1. *To construct the purse base, follow the same directions that were used for the base in the Tissue Birdhouse Box (see page 94). Use these dimensions:*

- Thread the top and bobbin with Sulky White Bobbin Thread.

- Fold 12 feet of cord in half and use a medium-width, short-length zig-zag to sew them together.

- Fold in half again and zig-zag them together (4 cords across).

- Cut four 8-3/4" pieces from the 4-cord strip and stitch them together to construct the 16-cord base (it should measure 3").

- Trim both ends straight to reach an 8-1/2" length.

- To give it strength and stability, iron a piece of **Sulky Fuse 'n Stitch** (shiny side down) that is slightly less than 3" x 8-1/2" onto each side of your rectangular base.

Base uncovered

- Fuse two 4" x 9-1/2" pieces of Steam-A-Seam2 onto the wrong side of the fabric you have chosen for your purse bottom. To fuse the fabric onto the 3" x 8-1/2" base, follow the directions for the Birdhouse on page 89 so that both the front and back are covered.

2. Wrap the clothesline with 1" wide strips of fabric, following the "Clothesline Wrapping Instructions" on page 90.

3. Thread the top and bobbin with a Sulky 30 wt. Blendables thread that coordinates with your selected fabric. Select a multiple zig-zag stitch with a medium length and width. Begin attaching the wrapped cord to the covered base at one corner, leaving the end to hang slightly past the corner as it tends to pull back just a bit, and the very end is mostly fabric that will compress.

4. To construct the purse, follow the base instructions on page 94. After doing the first two rows flat, hold the base at an angle to your machine to achieve the curved appearance of the purse sides for a total of 28 rows.

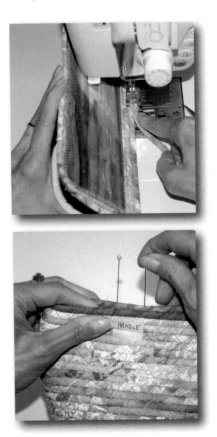

Shoulder Bag

5. After 28 rows, stop in the front center and change to your bottom base fabric; wrap one more row and remove it from the machine. Do not cut the wrapped cord. Fold the purse in half and mark approximately 2" from the side fold for handle placement. Place a 1" piece of masking tape to the right of the 2" mark on each **inside** of the purse, exactly across from each other. Find the center back of the purse (across from your color change) and mark it for your button loop placement.

6. Put the purse back under the presser foot and continue zig-zagging on the wrapped cord. When you come to your first 1" tape, **STOP**, bartack several times, jump over the tape (leaving a 1" opening), bartack again, then resume zig-zagging on the wrapped cord.

7. When you get to the mark for the loop placement, pull up the loop size (about 8") that will fit your button. Continue zig-zagging along the 8" loop only, without connecting it to the

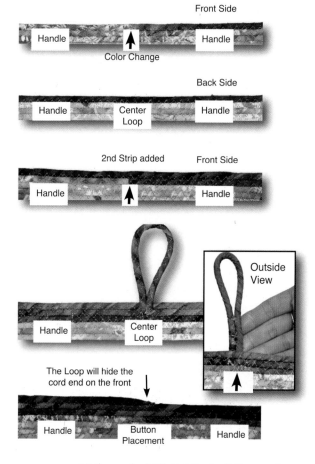

View of Purse's top edge (color change)

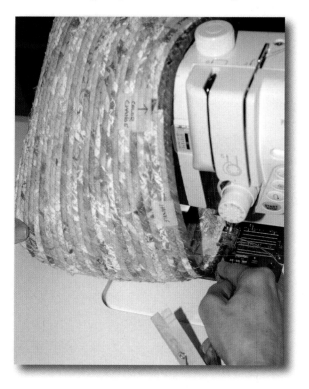

purse. At the end of 8", tightly butt the cord into the loop base and continue sewing.

8. Repeat, **jumping over the tape,** as you reach each 1" base opening for the other 3 handle positions. Continue to zig-zag for one more row, **placing the last row under the loop as you come to it.**

9. At the center front of your purse, finish with a tapered end at the point where you started your color change. If you need to tighten the loop to fit your button, zig-zag the two sides together, up from the base.

Purse Handles:

- Cut 2 - 4" x 31" strips of fabric.

- Cut 2 - 4" x 30" strips of **Sulky Fuse 'n Stitch Stabilizer**.

- Fuse the shiny side of **Fuse 'n Stitch** to the wrong side of the fabric, leaving 1/2" of fabric at each end to be folded over the **Fuse 'n Stitch** for a more finished look.

- Fold in half the length of the fabric and press.

- Unfold and fold both long sides to the center seam and press.

- Then, fold in half and press flat to equal a 1" wide handle.

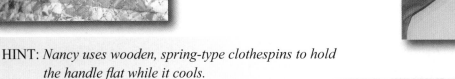

1. Straight stitch or decorative stitch along both long edges of the handle. Insert the handle into the purse slot from the front to the inside *(one handle per side of purse)*. Fold extra fabric to the inside.

HINT: *Nancy uses wooden, spring-type clothespins to hold the handle flat while it cools.*

2. Attach a zipper foot, select a straight stitch, and move your needle all the way to the right or left needle position. Stitch the handle as close to the purse as possible. Do this on all four handle attachments. Use a permanent fabric glue to glue the remaining inside flap flat to the handle, and secure it with a clothespin until dry.

   This process makes some lovely handles that hold up nicely. If the handles do become misshapened, re-shape them by ironing. **Sulky Fuse 'n Stitch** becomes soft when heat is applied, so they are easy to re-shape.

3. Sew on your decorative button and *enjoy your fun purse!*

Shoulder Bag

Loose Ends Scarf

by Diane Gloystein, National Sulky Educator

"Sulky Blendables look as though you artfully hand-dyed the thread in magnificent hues! I love the rich color combinations, the smooth perfection, and the very high quality of Blendables threads!" --- Diane

Instructions for this **"Bonus Project"** can be found on the CD in the back of this book.

Decorative Stitched Bag

by *Lee Fletcher* – *National Sulky Educator & Designer*

"I love the Blendables on black fabric because the color transitions in the Blendables really stand out. I also love combining different color combinations of the Blendables. The thickness of the thread complements the decorative stitches for a unique design on this little bag." --- Lee

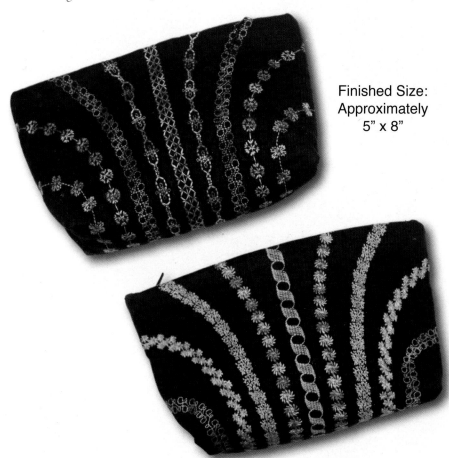

**Finished Size:
Approximately
5" x 8"**

Lee has been involved in costume making for Ballet. She owned her own manufacturing company which produced her designs, and now she owns "Fletcher Ross Designs" which produces sewing patterns that are skill builders for quilters and non-quilters alike. She supports her customers by teaching classes. Lee has also enjoyed an extensive career in Sales Management for consumer product companies.

Visit her at:
www.pat-e-patterns.com

Instructions for this **"Bonus Project"** can be found on the CD in the back of this book.